D1327295

Robert Bolling
Woos Anne Miller

Love and Courtship in Colonial Virginia, 1760

Robert Bolling Woos Anne Miller

Love and Courtship in Colonial Virginia,

1760

Edited by

J. A. LEO LEMAY

University Press of Virginia
Charlottesville and London

THE UNIVERSITY PRESS OF VIRGINIA
Copyright © 1990 by the Rector and Visitors
of the University of Virginia

First published 1990

Library of Congress Cataloging-in-Publication Data
Bolling, Robert, b. 1738.
Robert Bolling woos Anne Miller : love and courtship in Colonial
Virginia, 1760 / edited by J. A. Leo Lemay.
p. cm.
Letters from Bolling's manuscript journal-epistle entitled "A
circumstantial account of certain transactions that once greatly
interested the writer . . ." and his poems about the courtship.
Includes bibliographical references (p.   ).
ISBN 0-8139-1259-8
1. Virginia—Social life and customs—Colonial period, ca.
1600-1775. 2. Courtship—Virginia—History—18th century.
3. Bolling. Robert, b. 1738—Correspondence. 4. Virginia—
Biography. I. Lemay, J. A. (Joseph A. Leo), 1935- . II. Title.
F229.B68   1990
975.5'58202'092—dc20
[B]   89-27362
                                                            CIP

Printed in the United States of America

Contents

Acknowledgments

When I visited the Research Department of Colonial Williamsburg, Inc., in May 1980, John Ingram, Curator of Special Collections, mentioned that a hitherto-unknown manuscript by Robert Bolling had been found in the unprocessed papers of the Tucker-Coleman Collection at the College of William and Mary. I promptly went to the Swem Library at the college, where Margaret Cook, Curator of Manuscripts, found Bolling's "Circumstantial Account" for me and later made a photocopy of it and gave me permission to publish it. I am most grateful to Mr. Ingram and Miss Cook. In 1968, for my first essay on Bolling, Richard Henneman and his brother John B. Henneman allowed me to purchase a microfilm of Bolling's manuscript volume "Hilarodiana," and the Huntington Library, San Marino, California, supplied me with Xerox copies of the Bolling manuscript volumes in its possession. I am once again indebted to the Hennemans and the Huntington Library for these copies and for permission to publish from them. In June 1988 John M. Hemphill and Cathy Hellier of the Research Department of Colonial Williamsburg read a draft of the completed manuscript and gave me the benefit of their suggestions. And I am indebted to Jon Kukla and Brent Tarter of the Virginia State Library and Archives who assisted my research there in July 1988. Professor Edward A. Nickerson of the University of Delaware has translated several passages of Bolling's Italian at my request. My research assistant Thomas J. Haslam has helped in every phase of the research for this book. My research assistant Darin Fields has proofread the pages and has compiled the index.

Robert Bolling
Woos Anne Miller

Love and Courtship in Colonial Virginia, 1760

Introduction

Robert Bolling's journal-epistle, which he entitled "A Circumstantial Account of Certain Transactions, that once greatly interested the Writer . . ." recounts his courtship of Anne ("Nancy") Miller from January to September 16, 1760. The seventeen poems also printed here complement the journal, which was not composed until after the courtship was over. Bolling and Miller lived in the Petersburg area of Virginia, on the Appomattox River, just above its juncture with the James. Bolling limited his journal to the interactions between himself and Anne Miller, giving only incidental references to the places, circumstances, and other persons involved in the courtship. A complete diary of Bolling's life from January to September 1760 would contain far more information. Bolling did not, for example, mention the marriage of his brother John on June 24, 1760, to Mary Jefferson (Thomas Jefferson's sister), though he surely attended the wedding. (Evidently Anne Miller did not go to the wedding—or Bolling would have included it.) Though we may regret that Bolling did not keep a full record of all his activities during 1760, "A Circumstantial Account" has a single focus and thus is more structured as a narrative and consequently more interesting as a story than most journals.

In subject matter, the seventeen poems that complement the journal are surprisingly modern, for they invite comparison to the personal poetry that emerged in the 1960s as a dominant new kind of modern poetry, associated especially with W. D. Snodgrass and the late Robert Lowell. Though post–World War II personal poetry is more introspective than Bolling's, it resembles eighteenth-century "occasional verse" (i.e., poetry about specific occasions), describing the writer's experiences and emotions. One major difference between the two is that Bolling deliberately attempted to compare his personal experiences to classical and contemporary literary paradigms, whereas post-Romantic writers prize the uniqueness of their experience.

Besides being interesting as literature, Bolling's "Circumstantial Account" reveals the actual courtship behavior of wealthy colonial Virginians more fully than any other single surviving source. It also shows the social whirl of courtship-age colonial Virginia aristocrats, valuably supplementing such well-known diaries of colonial Virginia as William Byrd's and Landon Carter's.[1] It provides a key into the character of the author, who was the dominant poet and writer of pre-Revolutionary Virginia. And finally, the journal sheds incidental light upon a number of people and upon the details of life-style in the colonial South.

COURTING

Courtship among the colonial Virginia gentry centered around dancing.[2] Officers of Rochambeau's army present in Williamsburg in the winter of 1781–82 noted, "There are endless balls; the women love dancing."[3] In his journal Bolling specifically mentioned two balls (as the more formal gatherings for dancing were called): one on Wednesday, February 13, 1760, at Blandford, "a Ball, made by herself [Anne Miller] and Betsy Stark," and one on Friday, February 22, when he was Anne Miller's partner at "a second Ball." Several additional courtship scenes clearly took place at dances. Bolling noted that on Thursday, January 17, at Herbert Haynes's home, "Somebody very opportunely led her [Anne Miller] out to dance." The entertainment at Bob Walker's where the group spent the night, Monday, January 14, and where "Miss Miller was my Partner," evidently featured dancing. It seems likely that Bolling and Miller were dancing on Saturday night, January 12, at Badwington, when Bolling, intoxicated, amazed the company by seizing Anne Miller, kissing "her a thousand Times," and proposing to her. Indeed, the four-day excursion from Saturday, January 12, to Tuesday, January 15, probably featured dancing every night. Bolling asserted that during that period, his "Transports were so great, that I scarce felt any of that Lassitude, which generally attends long Watching and great Exercise." The characterization "long Watching," i.e., staying up late, and "great Exercise" seems particularly apt as a description of dancing.[4]

In the eighteenth century dancing was a necessary social grace and a mark of social standing. Philip Fithian, the Princeton graduate who tutored Robert Carter III's children in 1773–74, continually betrayed his excruciating embarrassment over his inability to dance. He confided to his journal that in Virginia, dancing was "a necessary qualification for a person to appear even decent in Company!"[5] The Carter children, like most wealthy young Virginians, were taught dancing and music by special tutors.[6] At the beginning of 1782, a Pennsylvania line officer, visiting a North Carolina family with numerous Bolling connections, described the progress of various dances in a single evening:

> In the evening the Ball was opened by a Minuet with each lady in the room; which is the custom here; that done we stood up for Country Dances; from that to Reels, and then to Jiggs. In the Minuet the Ladies here excell; Country Dances they don't understand well; Reels they Dance well enough, but Jiggs is their favorites. 'Tis customary for the gentlemen after the Jigg to Kiss their Partners, and nothing but that could have induced me to dance the Jiggs; for you know I'm not fond of them. We continued dancing 'till about 4 o'clock in the morning, when the Ladies retired and the gentlemen set in for drinking and mischief, making a noise that kept the whole house awake, pulling those out of bed who attempted to sleep.[7]

Because southern (even aristocratic) white children sometimes danced with black children when the elders were not looking (the Princeton tutor Philip Fithian recorded this fact with horror), the jigg in colonial Virginia seems to have been influenced by Afro-American dance traditions.[8] Both Andrew Burnaby, who traveled in Virginia in 1759–60, and Nicholas Cresswell, who witnessed a dance on January 7, 1775, wrote that they perceived the influence of black dancing styles upon Virginia versions of jigs.[9]

The ability to dance, with style and grace, the formal court dances of England and Europe indicated one's background and training. On December 28, 1727, the new Virginia governor William Gooch with relief reassured his brother Thomas in England that Virginians were highly civilized and well accomplished: "The Gentlemen and Ladies here are perfectly well bred, not an ill Dancer in my Government." [10] Celebrating the deceased governor Benedict Leonard Calvert (d. 1732) as an ideal eighteenth-century gentleman, the Maryland poet Richard Lewis thought it important to describe his dancing:

> When Gaily dress'd, to Grace the Publick Ball,
> He to soft Musick mov'd around the Hall;
> His Artful Step, his Unaffected Air,
> His Easy Grandeur, Charm'd the Circling Fair:
> Each Dancer his Superior Skill Confess'd,
> And Pleasure Glow'd in each Spectator's Breast
> (ll. 125–30) [11]

Dancing was popular throughout all ranks of society, though minuets were generally reserved for the more formal balls. Diarists noted who were the best dancers, [12] and one abysmal record exists of a 1760 fight between two Maryland tenant farmers caused by "some Bickerings about their skill in Dancing a Jigg." [13]

Robert Bolling's "Circumstantial Account" reveals the emotions (and some of the actions) of a young man in love. It is the most detailed colonial American courtship account told from a young man's viewpoint. Previous scholarly accounts necessarily have been based upon etiquette books and other surviving records. Eighteenth-century Virginia ladies were hardly frank in their discussion of courtship; and most surviving evidence, from both letters and diaries, is by women. Until now, the best-known male colonial courtship account was Samuel Sewall's 1720 courtship of Madame Katharine Winthrop, but Boston's Judge Sewall was sixty-eight at the time and the twice-widowed Winthrop was fifty-six. The courtship's physical highpoint occurred when Sewall took off one of Winthrop's gloves, because, he said, "twas great odds between handling a dead Goat, and a living Lady." [14] One colonial historian has commented that "erotic passion" is "conspicuously absent" from the extant literary evidence. [15] The ladies thought erotic language indecorous. On November 5, 1782, Lucinda Lee noted that the poetry of Alexander Pope's "Eloisa to Abelard" was "beautiful," but she did "not like some of the sentiments." The language and feeling expressed by Eloisa were "Too Ammorous for a female, I think."[16] Edmund S. Morgan has concluded that convention demanded the marriage proposal "take place in an atmosphere of almost religious formality." He stated further: "The lady must be approached with fear and trembling as a kind of saint, the lover prostrating himself either literally or figuratively before her."[17] Nevertheless, other evidence besides Bolling's journal testifies that courting couples were comparatively free in colonial Virginia. Indeed, one French officer disapprovingly commented on the lack of chaperonage in Revolutionary Virginia: "when a girl has chosen her 'beau,' she is free to shut herself up with him for hours on end."[18]

In "A Circumstantial Account," Bolling pointed out the different attractions of different women. Mary Herbert Claiborne "had a fine shape, some Sense and more Beauty, with a great Share of what the French call Douceur." Her body, beautiful face, mind, and personality were all appealing, and Bolling added that he "cou'd scarce avoid being pleased with so pretty a creature." From one of his poems (no. 2) we learn that Elizabeth Starke was quite short and from another (no. 10) that she was "ripe for a mate." His love, Anne Miller, presumably was not so striking as Mary Claiborne: "Her Person was genteel and the Turn of her Face agreeable, tho not beautiful." In a poem (no. 4, l. 25), he referred to Anne Miller's "greyhound Form and Lamia face," so we can suppose that she was slender and muscular, with a deceptively appealing face. Bolling was attracted to her first by her personality, especially "a Sprightliness in every Thought and Action." He commented, however, that she occasionally behaved like a spoiled child: "She had a Haughtiness, I may even say, a Fierceness in her Countenance; which, on any little Emotion, destroyed, in some Degree, that pretty Softness, which is so amiable in a young Lady." But her mind more than made up for her disposition: "With this Violence of Temper she had a Fund of good Sense, which served as a Counterpoise to that Defect: and which, as she grew older, seemed intirely to have mastered it."

Though Bolling found a beautiful face and form worth comment, and though he thought personality and good sense were important, the emotional feelings and erotic passion were, for him, most important. Bolling declared, "I found it impossible to have this Lady in my Arms for Hours together, without feeling such Emotions, as are the unavoidable Consequence of much Familiarity between the Sexes." But it was Anne Miller—not any other young lady with whom he danced for hours—who especially aroused Bolling. "The pleasing Passion insensibly wrought itself into my Constitution, and became as much a Necessity with me as Hunger, Thirst, or any other involuntary Inclination." Finally, he lost his mind in public: "Forgetting every Thing, I gave Way to the Impulses of my Passion. I seized the dear Creature to my Bosom, kissed her a thousand Times," and proposed marriage.

Of course, Bolling was trained in the courtship customs of the English and American gentry. (While at school in England, he spent vacations at his relations' country homes.) He realized that his behavior was not traditionally proper; in telling his correspondent of the emotions he felt upon holding "this Lady in my Arms for Hours together," he explained that "the great Intimacy, between Relations in this Colony, permitting many Freedoms," he could not help himself.

Bolling recorded several times when the lovers obviously spent considerable time kissing, caressing, and enjoying prolonged close contact. Bolling's purpose was certainly not to kiss and tell. He did not dwell on these occasions, and he gave no amorous details, but no one can doubt from the implicit evidence that intimate caresses took place. On January 31, "as my Nancy was generally on a bed with me, I had sufficient Opportunity to represent the Violence of my Passion." And on February 26, he "did indeed endeavour to behave to her with Indifference; but, coming by Accident into a Chamber, where she was sitting, extremely pensive, on a *Bed:* I cou'd no longer withhold, but overcome by an Excess of Passion, I threw myself *thereon*, and pressed her to my Bosom, with a Rapture, which can scarce be conceived. She reproached me with (but my Answers convinced her, I had no) Coldness. While we were together on the Bed I overlaid and broke a Fan of hers: a Necklace too had already fallen a Sacrifice to my Caresses."

Besides these two occasions, one must believe that the young lovers spent time kissing and caressing at Grenock on July 16, on various occasions from August 26 (when Anne Miller wrote her father that she had "fixed my Affections on Mr. Bolling") to September 4 (when Bolling said

"I really was in Extacies"), and finally on September 14 when Bolling went with Anne Miller to her room at Mitchels after the family had gone to bed and at last "took Leave after the warmest Embraces." Most past literary documentation of courtship among the eighteenth-century gentry of England and America would suggest that sustained kissing, caressing, and embracing between courting couples was exceptional. But common sense, statistical surveys of pregnancy at marriage, human nature, and now Bolling's journal testify that such courtship practices existed throughout colonial Virginia society.[19]

In addition to passion, lust, and love, another human emotion was common in eighteenth-century courtships—jealousy. Twice Bolling deliberately flirted with other young ladies in order to make Anne Miller jealous. The first time was on January 31, at Broadway, when Elizabeth Starke began the game by encouraging him in order to make her suitor, Carter Harrison, jealous. Bolling recorded: "We had each the Success proposed. Carter seemed at the Gates of Death: the Agitation of Nancy Miller sufficiently evinced that, if she had but little Esteem for me, she had at least a Quantity of self-Love, that cou'd ill-brook the Loss of an Admirer." That scene was followed by a night of reconciliation and passion between Bolling and Miller. (The poem addressed to Elizabeth Stark [no. 2, below], after Bolling spent the night in her bed while she was away, suggests that his flirtation had some basis.)

The second occasion was on June 6. Because Anne Miller had behaved coldly to him the last time he saw her, Bolling was "a good Deal" piqued and "took great Pains to tickle her Bosom with that pleasant Passion Jealousy." He therefore embraced Mary Herbert Claiborne "with Transport" but Anne Miller coldly. Finally Anne Miller exclaimed "*Such Scenes!* and soon after withdrew." Although the journal-epistle testifies primarily to Bolling's chagrin and unhappiness over the course and the outcome of the courtship, the period was not without flirtatious satisfactions for him, both with and without Anne Miller. Bolling's consciousness of his and other people's psychology is frequently present in the journal and makes one acknowledge the timelessness of human emotions. When Bolling reported that Anne Miller "gave no other than evasive Answers, expressing Doubts of my Sincerity and Apprehensions of her father's Disapprobation," and then commented, "Nothing cou'd be more encouraging than this kind of Behavior," every reader must smile at this age-old tactic and response.

Bolling conceded that he violated the formal customs of eighteenth-century courtship by informing Anne Miller's father "by Message, of my Intentions." He said, "Some People censured" him for not immediately going to see Hugh Miller and "acquainting him with it myself." This statement has a revealing omission and consequent ambiguity. Although Bolling granted that he should have gone to see Hugh Miller, he stated that the purpose of the visit would have been to inform Miller of his intentions. But he also should have said that he was asking Hugh Miller's permission to marry his daughter; he undoubtedly did so in the message.

Instead, Bolling implied that the decision to marry was wholly up to Anne Miller and himself. As subsequent events proved, however, the marriage decision depended also upon Hugh Miller's consent—which, in turn, was evidently influenced by his close friend and adviser James Johnson. So the role of the parents was, as the secondary literature would lead us to expect, more important in the eighteenth century than today.[20] The parents might have had an even more important role in the courtship between Robert Bolling and Anne Miller except that both lovers had already lost one parent. Bolling's father had died in 1757 and Miller's mother in 1756 or 1757.

Bolling's omission of the information that he asked Hugh Miller's permission to wed his daughter reveals a dominant aspect of his character. He was obviously proud and independent. Even after the courtship was over and Anne Miller had left Virginia, Bolling was unwilling to admit to himself his initial mistake (and to write it down)—he should have gone personally to ask Hugh Miller's permission to wed his daughter. Instead he hurriedly glossed over the episode. Bolling did not want, even in retrospect, to put himself in the submissive posture of asking Hugh Miller's permission.

The omission dovetails with his character as it is revealed throughout the journal and his other writings. Bolling could have decided to accompany the Millers to Scotland in 1760. He had Hugh Miller's promise that if he did go with them and if the lovers still wanted to marry one another in two years' time, then Hugh Miller would give them his blessing. Bolling did not record the fact that his mother did not want him to leave Virginia; that information comes out indirectly. In proving that James Johnson was the archvillain of the story, Bolling quoted a letter from his cousin Bolling Starke of September 7, 1760, asking if "your Mother's Reconciliation to your leaving her" could be gained. The proud young Bolling did not want to acknowledge to himself or to others the key roles played by Anne Miller's father and by his own mother. Bolling's pride generally seems to be a not exaggerated sense of his own proper dignity and value. It usually seems to be a due self-respect. But he seems to deny—by his omissions—a proper sense of the parents' traditional role in the eighteenth century and to be unable to state his deference to the parents.

The persons mentioned as present during the courtship were for the most part of a courting age. The ladies were mainly mid-teenagers and the men generally in their early twenties. Anne Miller became seventeen in 1760; Mary Bolling became sixteen; Mary Herbert Claiborne became fifteen; and Elizabeth Starke, sixteen. The young men present at the dances or mentioned as rivals were older: Bolling became twenty-two in 1760; Jerman Baker evidently became twenty-five; Theodorick Bland (whose involvement was two years later) became eighteen; Carter Henry Harrison became twenty-four; Abner Nash, twenty; Peyton Skipwith, twenty; Bolling Starke, twenty-seven; and Robert Walker, thirty-one. The ages of the courting couples dovetails with those given in the standard scholarly literature: the average age for courting—and for marriage—was younger for women during the eighteenth century than it is today.[21]

The comparatively young age of the courting women no doubt partially explains why the role of the parent was especially important then. Hugh Miller evidently thought his daughter was too young to marry. All he asked was that the couple wait two years. Of course, he knew that two years is a long time for young courting adults. Further, Anne Miller, Robert Bolling, and their circle were all wealthy. If Hugh Miller had disowned his daughter, that would have made a great impact upon her standard of living. Because Bolling's father was dead, the poet had already received his inheritance, and he was presumably his own master; yet he too was influenced by his parent. Although Elizabeth Blair Bolling does not seem to have opposed the marriage, she did not want him to leave Virginia again.

During the courtship and especially after it, Bolling was occasionally bitter and resentful. Certainly the tone of the letter he wrote to Anne Miller (quoted in the conclusion of the journal) on September 30 is extremely bitter. And on one occasion he revealed a sexism characteristic of the eighteenth century. On September 4 Bolling measured Anne Miller's "wedding Finger" and "ordered a Ring to be made." Then, on September 5, she received word from her father once again: he was "much displeased" that the two lovers had been seeing one another. Therefore, "after weeping in the most affectionate Manner," she asked Bolling to relinquish his courtship and see her no more. Bolling became furious and left "without taking Leave." In the journal he argued that according to civil law, consent and not cohabitation (i.e., living together and having sexual intercourse) makes a marriage. Therefore, "she owed me more Duty, as her Husband, than she did her Father." To him, Anne Miller had no occasion for her own sense of self-worth but should have been dutiful first to her father and then to her would-be husband.

Written in anger, Bolling's journal reflects the highest pitch of his wounds. But there can be no doubt of Bolling's pride (a pride that was said by contemporaries to characterize Virginians) [22] and of his resentment. He himself recognized his pride. In a "Letter to Jerman Baker" (poem no. 14), he told of a lady's anger with him. Bolling said that he was therefore angry in turn with her, but if she would banish all acid from her dealings with him, then he would do so too. Until then, "I have my Nature, Sir, / As well as she" (ll. 38–39). The "Circumstantial Account," written in anger, self-justification, and bitterness, well reveals the pride of a colonial Virginia aristocrat.

Courtship and marriage involved the entire community more in the eighteenth century than today. Friends and relations were drawn into the courtship as advisers, intermediaries, and advocates. Even the proud, independent Robert Bolling used his cousin Bolling Starke and his uncle Alexander Bolling as his advocates with Hugh Miller. Presumably his mother too supported her son's endeavor. She must have hosted the "little Entertainment" at Cobbs on February 26 that Hugh and Anne Miller and James Johnson attended. Of course, Bolling's main advocate with

Anne Miller was his best friend, Jerman Baker. Indeed, Baker sought her out so frequently and talked with her at such length that their friends and relations began to suspect a Priscilla Alden response from Anne Miller—Speak for yourself, Jerman. But the evidence that Baker courted her for himself was illusory. He remained Bolling's advocate and adviser. Finally, if Bolling's evidence has any validity, the person who really opposed and ultimately prevented the marriage was Hugh Miller's friend and adviser James Johnson.

THE SETTING

As Benjamin Franklin remarked, "The Golden Age never was the present age."[23] Certainly colonial Virginians living in 1760 did not believe that they were living in a golden age, though some later writers have imagined that it was. During the middle of the eighteenth century, after many of the great Georgian houses had been built, and before the Stamp Act crisis of 1765 began the inexorable drift toward the Revolution, Virginia enjoyed a period of political, cultural, and economic flourishing. By 1760, during Robert Bolling's courtship of Anne Miller, the British had turned the tide of the French and Indian War (1754–63). Quebec had fallen in 1759, and the French surrendered Canada in 1760. The Virginia frontier was relatively quiet. George Washington (who became twenty-eight in 1760) resigned his commission in 1759. Thomas Jefferson, a youth of seventeen, went down to Williamsburg early in 1760 to begin his first year at the College of William and Mary.

Williamsburg, generally a sleepy town, became a bustling center whenever the General Assembly met. Governor Francis Fauquier called three sessions of the Virginia assembly in 1760: March 4–11, May 19–24, and October 6–20. On March 4 Fauquier announced the appointment of General Jeffery Amherst, commanding general of the British forces fighting in America, as the absentee governor of Virginia. On May 19 Fauquier asked the assembly to raise more men for the Virginia Regiment (then commanded by William Byrd III, age thirty-one) because fighting had broken out again with the Cherokees, especially on the southwestern frontier. And on October 6 Fauquier again asked the assembly for more men to bring the Virginia Regiment up to full strength.[24]

Because Bolling recorded that he visited Gloucester County sometime between February 27 and April 27, and because the most convenient road
from Petersburg to Gloucester passed through Williamsburg, it seems
probable that Bolling stayed in Williamsburg for the first meeting of the
assembly, March 4–11, taking the opportunity to see friends and hear
the news. His poem to William Starke (no. 10) proves that he was in
Williamsburg in October, probably for some or all of the third session of
the legislature, October 6–20.

Williamsburg, though occasionally a scene of importance for the
ordinary Virginia planter, was not normally the dominant center of colonial Virginia life. The map Bolling drew at the beginning of his journal
focuses upon the most significant ordinary features of colonial Virginia
life—the rivers, counties, and great houses. The rivers were the main
routes of transportation, trade, and communication in early America, and
therefore on their banks were the houses. Most places mentioned in the
journal are located on Bolling's map. The rivers were also obstacles and
logical boundary lines in colonial America. Except for Cobbs and the vil-
lage of Pocahontas, all the places shown on the map are located on the
south side of the Appomattox and the James rivers, from Petersburg and
Blandford in the west, above the falls of the Appomattox, to Flower-
de-Hundred (or Flowerdew Hundred) in the east, a deepwater port (in
eighteenth-century terms) on the James River.[25]

Bolling also carefully marked the counties of Dinwiddie, Prince
George, Chesterfield, Henrico, and Charles City on his map. The counties were the most essential units in colonial Virginia culture. Military,
religious, political, legal, and even social structures were organized along
county lines. The primary symbol of the county structure was the county
court. Its justices, generally numbering between fourteen to twenty-five,
were the dominant gentry (and largest landowners) in the county. Fairs
and social gatherings took place around its monthly meetings. The itiner-
ant lawyers went from one county court to another to practice law; the
meeting days were deliberately staggered in order to allow the lawyers to
attend four to ten different county courts a month. Election to the House
of Burgesses was apportioned by county. The Virginia militia was organized by county. And often, there was but one parish per county; in that

case, its boundaries were synonymous with the county's.[26] Bolling located the Prince George County courthouse on his map.

The third feature that dominates Bolling's map are the great houses—synonymous with the families of colonial Virginia. The family houses, the primary scenes where the courtship took place, are indicated on the map. Many of them were old when Bolling was courting Anne Miller. Bolling's map lists three more family homes on the south side of the rivers than appeared on the Joshua Fry and Peter Jefferson map of 1751: Grenock, J. Murray, and Mitchels.[27] On the other hand, Bolling omitted the places not mentioned in his journal, and thus a number of famous family homes on the north side of the rivers are absent, including the Richard Randolphs' family home, Curles; the Cockes' family home, Bremo; and Randolphs' Turkey Island; the Carters' Shirley; and the Byrds' Westover. Most of the plantation houses that Bolling mentioned, like Cobbs, were wooden structures (Mitchell's was an exception). The fate of Cobbs was typical. It passed out of the family hands in 1827, the surrounding trees were lumbered off, the house itself, uninhabited, fell into ruin, the family graveyard was despoiled by livestock, and finally Federal troops burned the old structure in 1864.[28]

ROBERT BOLLING AND ANNE MILLER

Anne Miller and Robert Bolling were both great-grandchildren of Colonel Robert Bolling (1646–1709), the emigrant, but Bolling descended from the Colonel's first wife, Jane Rolfe Bolling (the granddaughter of Pocahontas and John Rolfe), and Miller descended from his second wife, Anne Stith Bolling. Bolling was four years and eight months older than Anne Miller. In January 1760, when the journal begins, Bolling was twenty-one and Anne Miller was sixteen. She became seventeen on March 24, 1760, and five months later (August 28, 1760), he became twenty-two.

Anne ("Nancy") Miller was the daughter of Hugh and Jane Bolling Miller of Grenock. She was born on March 13, 1742/43, Old Style, and baptized at Blandford's Bristol Parish Church on April 10, 1743.[29] Anne Miller probably was tutored at home, perhaps with a few less well-to-do neighbors, according to the general practice among Virginia's gentry; with this same kind of education, her younger sister Jean became a litterateur and an intellectual.[30] After her mother's death in the winter of 1756–57, her father Hugh Miller, who had emigrated to Virginia from Scotland (no doubt as a tobacco factor), resolved to return to Glasgow. Her suitor, Robert Bolling, occasionally attended Bristol Parish Church (he left a satirical description of George Whitefield's preaching there in 1765),[31] and so the two young cousins no doubt saw one another at church as well as in the homes of mutual friends and relations in the Petersburg area. As Bolling's courtship journal makes abundantly clear, Anne Miller and he were part of the same group of young gentry involved in the social whirl of parties, dances, and entertainments in Chesterfield, Dinwiddie, and Prince George counties.

The Millers left Virginia on October 17, 1760. Theodorick Bland, Jr., in a letter written from Edinburgh, March 8, 1761, mentioned that "Mr. Hugh Miller and his family arrived in Glasgow about 2 or 3 months ago." Bland said that Hugh Miller "tells me he intends fixing his daughter Nancy at this place for some time, but is so infirm at present that he is uncertain when he shall be able to come here."[32] Probably during the summer of 1761, Hugh Miller moved the family to Edinburgh while he went to London, where he died on February 13, 1762.

By the fall of 1761 a courtship between Anne Miller and Bland, who was studying medicine at the University of Edinburgh, was flourishing. In 1762 Virginia rumors reported them married. Bolling's journal attests to the seriousness of the relationship. The antebellum Virginia historian Charles Campbell wrote that Bland's application to his medical studies "seems not to have monopolized his time so exclusively as to prevent him from falling into a love-affair, the object of which was a Miss Anne Miller—a young lady from Virginia who was then in Edinburgh. The scheme was strenuously opposed by his father, and his friend Dr. Fothergill, and was shortly afterwards abandoned. Indeed, young Bland himself in a letter disavows the affair, and sets it down as an unfounded surmise." The London merchant John Bland assured Theodorick in a letter of July 27, 1762, that he would "write thy good father on account of the report of thyself and Miss Miller, and doubt not that he will be eased from the [distress] he suffered on acc't of that report."[33]

Late in 1762 Peyton Skipwith, whom Bolling feared as a rival in 1760, voyaged to Edinburgh to woo Anne Miller. When Theodorick Bland, Jr., wrote his father in 1763, he said that he had "enjoy'd" Peyton Skipwith's company "for some days past." Bland added that he hoped Skipwith "will spend some time longer with us, at least I have conjectured so, as to all appearance there is an object in this place, who seems to engage his attention; but lest I should be wrong in my opinion, or premature in my intelligence, as happen'd to be the case lately with that convey'd with regard to myself, I shall be content with just having hinted it, as indeed I have no authority, nor sufficient appearance to do more; however time will show the event." Bland concluded the letter with a direct reference to Anne Miller: "Miss Miller who is in this town at present, and Mr. Peyton Skipwith, desire their best comp'ts to you and all their friends." [34]

Anne Miller and Peyton Skipwith (who did some sightseeing and then fell ill for several months) returned to Virginia in 1764, perhaps as a result of the news of Peyton's father's death on February 25 of that year. "About a fort'night after," they were married in Virginia. They lived briefly at Prestwould, Middlesex County; then at Greencrofts, on the Appomattox, Prince George County; and, after 1769, at Elm Hill, Mecklenburg County. In 1778, after Sir Peyton leased Hog Island, Surry County, from John Holt, they moved there. They had four children. First, Lelia (sometimes Lillias) (c. 1767–post 1792), who married, first, George Carter (1761–1788) of Shirley and, second (on October 8, 1791), St. George Tucker, a well-known writer and judge. [35] (The "Circumstantial Account" survives among the Tucker-Coleman Papers at the College of William and Mary.) Second, Grey (1771–1852), who inherited the estate of Sir Thomas Grey Skipwith (d. 1791) of Newbold Hall, England. Third, Maria, who died young. And fourth, Peyton (1779–1808) of Cotes, Georgia, who married Cornelia Lott Greene, daughter of General Nathanael Greene (1742–1786), on April 22, 1808. [36] Anne, Lady Skipwith, died at Hog Island, Surry County, on September 14, 1779, the day after the birth of her fourth child, Peyton.

Partly because of his numerous surviving manuscripts, much more is known about the life of Bolling. During his courtship of Anne Miller in 1760, Robert Bolling lived at Cobbs, on the Appomattox not far below

Petersburg. His paternal grandfather John Bolling I (1676–1729), a great-grandson of Pocahontas and John Rolfe, built the wooden mansion when the area was still a frontier. Returning from his expedition surveying the dividing line between North Carolina and Virginia, William Byrd II visited Cobbs in November 1728: "we arrived in the evening at Colonel Bolling's, where first from a primitive course of life we began to relapse into luxury. This gentleman lives within hearing of the falls of Appomattox River, which are very noisy whenever a flood happens to roll a greater stream than ordinary over the rocks." Byrd found the hospitality at Cobbs sumptuous. "We were entertained with much plenty and civility" and "fared sumptuously." [37]

A few months before Byrd's visit, John Bolling II (1700–1757) of Cobbs had married Elizabeth Blair, niece of the Reverend James Blair (1655–1743) and sister of John Blair (1687–1771), president of the Virginia Council and acting governor four times between 1758 and 1768. All of Bolling's male ancestors in Virginia except Thomas Rolfe served in the Virginia legislature. [38] Both Bolling's paternal grandfather and his father were wealthy and added greatly to their holdings by surveying [39] and by buying land. John Bolling I and his wife Mary Kennon Bolling had one son, John Bolling II, and five daughters: Jane (1702–1766), who married Colonel Richard Randolph (1690–1748) of Curles; Mary (1711–1744), who married Colonel John Fleming (1698–1756) of Mount Pleasant; Elizabeth (1709–c. 1766), who married Dr. William Gay (d. 1754?); Martha (1713–49), who married Thomas Eldridge; and Anne (1718–1800), who married James Murray of Athol Braes. William Stith, tracing the descendants of Pocahontas in his *History of Virginia* (1747), commented: "So that this Remnant of the Imperial Family of *Virginia,* which long ran in a single Person, is now encreased and branched out into a very numerous Progeny." Indeed, these five aunts supplied Robert Bolling with at least thirty first cousins, many of whom lived in the Petersburg area. [40] The Bollings and their kin were a prominent—and, finally, prolific—colonial Virginia family.

Robert Bolling was the third of eight children who lived to adulthood. He was born at Varina, then in Henrico County (now Chesterfield County), on August 17, 1738 (August 28, New Style). Evidently he displayed extraordinary scholastic ability as a child. The other children (including two older and two younger brothers and three younger sisters) were all tutored at home. The eldest son, Thomas Bolling (1735–1804), is said to have attended William and Mary and is known to have studied law in Williamsburg with Robert Carter Nicholas.[41] But only Robert was granted the privilege of an expensive English education. He sailed on the *Osgood*, Captain Wilkie, from Hampton on July 24, 1751, for London, where he arrived on September 3. He celebrated his thirteenth birthday on board the ship. The great Quaker tobacco merchant John Hanbury (1700–58) received the boy warmly, "as a man who esteemed his father." Hanbury sent him to the Grammar School of Queen Elizabeth at Wakefield, Yorkshire, a favorite school for Virginia boys, where he arrived on September 24.[42]

William Beverley of Blandfield, who had gone to England in 1750 to choose a school for his son and two other boys in his charge, welcomed him to Wakefield. Bolling joined a group of Virginians who were studying under the celebrated John Clarke, headmaster.[43] William Beverley had brought over Robert Beverley, to whom Bolling may have addressed his "Circumstantial Account" (he was the grandson of the Virginia historian); Robert Munford, the future playwright; and William Henry Fairfax, who in 1773 "died of a wound received at Montmorenci" and for whom Bolling wrote an elegy.[44] The inscribed books presented by departing students to the library of the grammar school indicate that several other Virginia boys attended school at Wakefield with Bolling: John Ambler presented a book in 1752; John Banister presented one in 1753; and both Thomas Smith and Theodorick Bland, Jr., did so in 1759. Other Virginia boys were studying at the nearby Heath Academy, just outside Wakefield. Edward Ambler and his brother John Ambler (who transferred in his last year to the Wakefield Grammar School), Augustin Smith, Richard Henry Lee, and Thomas Ludwell Lee were all at Heath during one or more of the five years that Bolling studied at Wakefield.[45]

Bolling made extraordinary progress in his studies, skipping several classes, and was put in with Beverley, Fairfax, and Munford. Shortly after being introduced to French, he "understood it better than the Latin, notwithstanding the great progress he had made in that language." His later fluency in Italian indicates that he probably had some formal training in that language; if so, it must have been at Wakefield.

Bolling also enjoyed the company of older English cousins who befriended him. During school vacations William Bolling of Ilkley invited the teenager to his home. Bolling recorded that he stayed there "five weeks on his first visit, and was there frequently afterwards." Here he met Elizabeth Bolling, who "altho twenty-five years of age entertained as much affection for our adventurer, as if he had been her own son." Bolling must have witnessed the courtship customs of the English gentry, for Elizabeth Bolling married William Prescott of Halifax while Bolling was in Yorkshire.[46] Bolling celebrated her memory (and the English seat of the Bolling family) by naming his Buckingham County home, built in 1760, Chellow, after a tract of land she possessed.

The English experience of most young Americans who were educated abroad entrenched them in an American identity. Americans were frequently shocked by the English ignorance of America and by the prejudice against it. William Byrd recorded his disgust for an English parson who thought that "Virginia was an Island lying without Ganges in the East Indies and that it was peopled first by a Colony sent thither by William Rufus."[47] Bolling was obviously bothered by English patronizing, for he recorded two versions of his grandfather's reply to typical English condescension.[48]

By 1755, when Bolling turned eighteen, he was pressing his father and other Virginians for the most recent political and military news. His friend John Banister, who left Wakefield in 1753, wrote on May 12, 1755, telling of George Washington's deeds and the progress of General Edward Braddock's army. His father wrote him on August 13 of Braddock's defeat.[49] On November 11, 1755, Bolling left Wakefield to return to Virginia. On the way, he visited London, where his cousin John Blair, Jr., was studying law at the Middle Temple. Bolling paid the fee, signed the register, and was admitted a member of the Middle Temple on December 31, 1755.[50] Two weeks later, January 14, 1756, he left for Gravesend, where he embarked on board the *Swift*, Captain Crookshanks, who had been second-in-command on the *Osgood* when Bolling sailed to England. "After a long voyage he arrived at York, on Good Friday," April 16, 1756.

Because the Virginia assembly was in session, Bolling did not go to Cobbs but to Williamsburg, where his father, a Chesterfield County burgess, received him. Evidently Bolling's father shared Middlesex County's John Smith's opinion of the law and of being a planter. Smith wrote on June 2, 1751, that "planting alone is poor doings, but with other business it will answer very well." Smith advised his young relations to go into law: "there is nothing surer as to profit," for "our Country pays a great sum yearly to diligent lawyers—and it increases daily." [51] John Bolling arranged to have his son Robert study law with Benjamin Waller. From the summer of 1756 to the fall of 1757, Bolling lived in Williamsburg, at George Davenport's house, just across the street from Waller's. [52] During that time he courted Susanna Chiswell, the daughter of Colonel John and Elizabeth Randolph Chiswell. Their courtship ended when she became engaged to Lewis Martin. After Bolling's father died on September 5, 1757, he gave up the study of law and moved back to Cobbs. [53] He lived there with his mother from 1758 to mid-1760, when he built a home at his plantation in Albemarle County (in an area that soon became Buckingham County). The Chiswell-Martin courtship failed, and his first flame Susanna Chiswell married Speaker John Robinson (1704–1766) in December 1759. [54]

John Bolling left his children well off. All five sons inherited large plantations. Robert Bolling's primary inheritance was an estate of more than 800 acres in Albemarle (later Buckingham) County, "near Willis's Mountains"; another on the James River near the Seven Islands; and a small tract called Toleres, a league farther up the James. John Bolling had 190 slaves and left each son 30. [55] Whatever the father's plans for the children, they went their own ways. Neither Bolling nor his brother Thomas made use of their legal studies, except for their service as justices in Buckingham and Chesterfield counties.

In February 1759 the London *Universal Magazine* published the first poem that I have identified as Bolling's. [56] Thereafter, he published poems frequently in various British magazines and in the colonial newspapers. [57] Unfortunately, the *Virginia Gazette*, where he often published from the mid-1760s to his death in 1775, has few extant issues from the period 1759 to 1765.

In March 1761 Albemarle County was divided, and two new counties, Buckingham and Amherst, were created from its southern section; the division became official on May 1, 1761. [58] The General Assembly of

1758–61 was dissolved on April 10, 1761; new elections were held during the summer of 1761. The twenty-three-year-old Robert Bolling was elected one of the two new delegates from Buckingham County. His name appears first on the report, indicating that he won the largest number of votes cast in the county. When the General Assembly of 1761–65 convened at Williamsburg on November 3, 1761, Bolling, along with the other burgesses, took the oaths of office. The assembly met first on Nov. 3–14, 1761, and then by successive prorogations on Jan. 14–21, March 30–April 7, Nov. 2–Dec. 21, 1762; May 19–31, 1763; Jan. 12–21, Oct. 30–Dec. 21, 1764; and May 1–June 1, 1765, when it was dissolved. Bolling seems to have attended faithfully.[59] On Nov. 4, 1762, he was appointed to the Committee on Propositions and Grievances; and on January 18–19, 1764, he served on an ad hoc committee which examined petitions of disabled veterans of Indian fighting.

About a year after Anne Miller left Virginia, Bolling began courting Mary Burton. On June 3, 1763, he took out a marriage license bond in Northampton County, with William Waters, of Williamsburg, as his security.[60] Mary Burton and he married at the "old Plantation," Northampton County, on the Eastern Shore, on June 5, 1763. Mary Burton, the daughter of William Burton III, was a major heiress. When her sister Margaret married Littleton Savage, Rind's *Virginia Gazette* of February 4, 1768, noted that she had "a Fortune of (at least) 10,000£." Bolling and his wife Mary had one child, Mary Burton Bolling, born at Jordan's, Prince George County, the home of Bolling's stepfather, Richard Bland. Two days later, May 2, 1764, Bolling's wife Mary died. Mary Burton Bolling (April 30, 1764–August 3, 1787) married Robert Bolling of Centre Hill, Petersburg, on November 4, 1781.

Bolling probably wrote his remarkable poem "Neanthe" while he was courting Mary Burton and spending considerable time on the Eastern Shore in 1763. Based upon Virginia history and folklore, "Neanthe" concerns one of the most disgusting sluts in American literature, the subject of a grotesque fight between her suitors. As part of the satire's background, Bolling featured "The Conjuror," Colonel Edmund Scarburgh (an infamous figure of mid-seventeenth-century Virginia history), who had numerous business dealings with the great-grandfather of Mary Burton. Bolling used Italian anti-Petrarchan traditions, eighteenth-century Virginia oral legends, and a traditional English form (Hudibrastic poetry) to create one of the most savage satires of American literature.[61]

Besides frequently writing poetry, Bolling wrote a series of prose pieces, including brief anecdotes.[62] An anecdote concerning the good manners of Governor William Gooch toward a slave appeared in the *London Magazine* of August 1764 under one of Bolling's common pseudonyms, "Varignano." Reprinted in the *Virginia Gazette* and the *Georgia Gazette*, it passed into the oral tradition and turned up in an American jestbook in 1795. Over a century later, the anecdote still circulated. In 1900 Booker T. Washington used the story as a "test of a true gentleman," though he attributed the courteous manners not to Gooch but to George Washington.[63]

Four lists of the Buckingham County justices of the peace survive from Bolling's lifetime. In the list of May 7, 1765, he is ranked sixth in a roster of nineteen. Evidently he had been appointed a justice when the county was created. On March 25, 1767, he was ranked third, but it was noted that he was then serving as sheriff of the county. On March 9, 1772, he was again ranked third. And in the last list taken during his life, June 27, 1774, he was second.[64] A disastrous fire destroyed almost all of the colonial records of Buckingham County,[65] but because both the county's 1773 list of tithes and his obituary give Bolling the title "Colonel," it is apparent that by 1773 he had become one of the three colonels of the Buckingham County militia (the colonel of the horse, the colonel of the foot, or the county lieutenant—the last being the chief officer of the county militia).

Bolling was present for the first part of the burgesses' meeting of May 1765, for he was added to the Committee on Propositions and Grievances on May 7, 1765. But, like many other burgesses, he evidently thought the pressing business of the session was over before the end of the month and thus left Williamsburg before Patrick Henry, on May 29, 1765, presented the Virginia Resolves against the Stamp Act. Bolling had important personal business planned for the month's end. Thirteen months after the death of his first wife, he remarried. Bolling posted a marriage bond in Amherst County, May 31, 1765: "Robert Bolling, Jr., bachelor, and Susanna Watson, spinster," with John Fraser as surety.[66] They were no doubt married early in June. The absence of any information concerning the family and lands of Susanna Watson suggests that she (unlike his first wife) was not from the dominant Virginia aristocracy. They had four children: Powhatan (1767–March 21, 1803), a member of the House of Delegates for Buckingham, 1798–99;[67] Pocahontas Rebecca (c. 1769–1803) who married, in 1783, Colonel Joseph Cabell (1762–1831); Elizabeth Blair (c. 1771–?), who married Major Thomas West (1751–1829), a member of the House of Delegates from Campbell County, 1799–1801, and son of Colonel John and Elizabeth Seaton West, of West Point; and Leneaus (1773–July 7, 1849), member of the House of Delegates for Buckingham, 1798–1800, 1810–11, and 1821–22, who married, December 16, 1793, Mary, daughter of Colonel Bernard and Mary Harris Markham.[68]

In the *Virginia Gazette* of June 20, 1766, Bolling precipitated a major crisis in colonial Virginia by questioning the General Court's bailment of Colonel John Chiswell, who had been arrested for the murder of Robert Routledge. Bolling suggested that the General Court had shown partiality toward Chiswell. In succeeding issues of the Virginia gazettes, the judges, their advisers, and various sycophants of the establishment defended the bailment, while Bolling, James Milner, Thomas Burke, and others attacked it. The Virginia newspapers for the latter half of 1766 were filled with writings about the case. In October 1766, the night before his trial, the defendant, father of Bolling's former girlfriend Susanna Chiswell Robinson, killed himself.

Colonel William Byrd III, one of the judges who allowed Chiswell bail, sued Bolling for libel; and John Wayles sued both Bolling and the printers of the Virginia newspapers for libel. On October 16, 1766, a grand jury was convened. Governor Francis Fauquier charged it to "punish the Licentiousness of the Press." The jury, however, "returned the said Indictments, NOT TRUE BILLS"; the verdict confirmed the existence of a free press in colonial Virginia.[69] Byrd then challenged Bolling to a duel, and honor dictated that Bolling accept. At 2 A.M. in the morning before the duel was to take place, Byrd and Bolling were arrested and jailed. Bolling carefully inquired into the origin of the arrests and learned that the shopkeeper from whom Byrd purchased the dueling pistols had alerted the authorities. The next day Byrd and Bolling were bound over to keep the peace. At the end of the year, Bolling published two poems satirizing his opponents in the quarrel and praising his friends.[70]

Under a variety of pseudonyms, Bolling dominated the poetry column of the *Virginia Gazette*. At the same time, he published more frequently in the London magazines than Arthur Lee, who was living in London.[71] Bolling generally was regarded as pre-Revolutionary Virginia's best writer—and as a primary defender of the rights and privileges of Virginians.[72] The Reverend Jonathan Boucher indirectly testified to Bolling's reputation, claiming in his autobiography that his own writings in the Chiswell case won him great popularity in 1766 and that the recollection of his role in the bailment was enough to save him from a patriot mob in 1775. It is clear, however, that Boucher had, at best, a minor role in the Chiswell affair and that Bolling was the major writer, followed by James Milner.[73]

When Governor Botetourt came to Virginia in 1768, Bolling parodied the welcoming ode that appeared in Rind's *Virginia Gazette* of November 3, 1768, and circulated the parody in manuscript. A few months later, he satirized the "Inundation of Addresses" that "flowed in upon our Governor, since his arrival" (Rind's *Gazette*, February 2, 1769). Naturally the government sycophants resented Bolling's writings: "Portius" replied to them in Rind's *Gazette* of March 16, 1769; and "R. S." brought up the matter again, after Botetourt's death, in the *Supplement* to Purdie and Dixon's *Virginia Gazette* of May 20, 1773.

On August 18, 1770, Bolling's younger brother Edward Bolling died in Amherst County, leaving Bolling his Buffalo Lick plantation and making the poet his executor. Bolling and his youngest brother Archibald disagreed over who was to receive the current crop from the Buffalo Lick plantation. Archibald hired George Wythe as his attorney and sued Robert Bolling for the crop. Bolling, the defendant, responded by engaging his brother-in-law Thomas Jefferson. Because the case was technically interesting, because Wythe and Jefferson were extraordinarily gifted attorneys, and because Bolling had some abstract interest in the law, he paid Thomas Jefferson an extra £5 for a complete record of the arguments in the case. Thus this minor dispute provides one of the most complete documents revealing Thomas Jefferson's abilities as a lawyer.[74]

Like several other Virginians, Bolling attempted to raise grapes and make wine. He read extensively about viniculture, experimented with growing different varieties of grapes, and wrote "An Essay on the Utility of Vine Planting in Virginia," in Purdie and Dixon's *Virginia Gazette* of February 25, 1773. He petitioned the House of Burgesses for "fifty Pounds sterling yearly, for the Term of five Years, in Order to enable him to prosecute his scheme of cultivating Grapes, for the making of Wine, which he is convinced, from Experiments, may be propagated in the upper parts of the Country." On March 11, 1773, Purdie and Dixon's *Virginia Gazette* noted that the House of Burgesses had directed the treasurer to pay Bolling the first of the annual payments. Bolling kept his friends abreast of his experiments with an article in Purdie and Dixon's *Gazette* of July 29, 1773.[75]

On March 4, 1773, Bolling published a long, ambitious poem on Virginia politics, "A Copy of Verses in Praise of Winter." It raised a major ruckus, partially because Bolling's contemporaries did not understand that it imitated an Italian classic; and replies to it appeared repeatedly in both Virginia gazettes until June 10. Robert Munford's response, "A Poem in Answer to One, Entitled 'The Winter Piece,'" remained in manuscript until 1798, when Munford's son published it in *A Collection of Plays and Poems*.[76]

Of the three extant lists of tithes for Buckingham County during Bolling's life, the 1764 enumeration contains the names of Bolling; an overseer, Thomas Jeffres; and eleven slaves: "America, Bristol, Tom, Lewey, Sifax, Bob, Jr., Hanah, Isabel, Maria, Hagar." To arrive at the listed total of thirteen tithes, "Bob, Jr.," must name two slaves. The report says that Bolling had no wheel carriages and no land, even though he had already inherited his lands in the county. The record for 1773 merely lists the number of "Col. Robert Bolling's Tiths by Order October Court" as twenty. The report of June 10, 1774, taken by George Hooper, is more detailed. It lists 809 acres, a chariot, and a chair and names the following servants and slaves: "William Shaw, Peter Roy, John Asher, Isabell, Betty, Moslea, Jenny, Hager, Lucey, Bristol, Lenee, Nelley, Nancy, Charles, Isaac, Salle, Jubiter, Jacob Staggltee, Joe, Jacob Cooper, Bounetts, Martin Jenney." The 1774 total gives Bolling twenty-five tithables.[77] Only three of the slaves from the 1764 list are also found in the 1774 list: Bristol, Hager, and Isabell; the others could have been at plantations he owned in other counties. To judge simply by the growth in the number of his tithes in Buckingham County, Bolling was gradually becoming wealthier.

On May 20, 1775, in Dixon and Hunter's *Gazette*, Bolling published his last major poem, an elegy on the deaths of a number of friends at the battle of Point Pleasant. Remnants of various poems on the battle survive from the oral tradition, and some of them echo portions of Bolling's lament. Of all the contemporary and later poems on this major battle of Dunmore's War, Bolling's is the longest, most detailed, and most interesting.[78]

In May 1775 Bolling returned to politics, running for a position in the Third Virginia Convention. He won (because his name is listed first, he evidently had more votes than John Nicholas, the other Buckingham County delegate) and was present in Richmond on July 17, 1775, when the convention met.[79] Abruptly and unexpectedly, Bolling died at Richmond, perhaps of a heart attack, on July 21, 1775, age 36. The obituary in Purdie's *Virginia Gazette* reported: "Last friday died suddenly, at Richmond, col. *Robert Bolling*, one of the delegates for Buckingham. He was a very amiable, polite, and accomplished gentleman, a firm patriot, and possessed abilities which rendered him an ornament to his country." George Gilmer wrote Thomas Jefferson the news: "Poor Bob Bolling has run his race, adieu to Burgundy, died suddenly at Richmond."[80]

In many ways Bolling was typical of the Virginia aristocracy of his day. He inherited wealth and a position of responsibility in the colony. Like his father and many of his cousins, he served as a justice of peace in the county court, as one of the three colonels of the Buckingham county militia; and as a member of the House of Burgesses and the Virginia Convention. He does not seem to have served on the vestry of Tillotson Parish, but that may have been because he had a low opinion of the minister.[81] There is every reason to believe that he would have been a leading politician of Revolutionary Virginia if he had not died at an early age. Bolling left a widow and five children.

What was extraordinary about Bolling was that he was the most accomplished litterateur of colonial Virginia. A pseudonymous correspondent, "Observator" (who must have been Pierre Etienne Du Ponceau),[82] sent in an "An Account of Two Americans of Extraordinary Genius in

Poetry and Music" to the *Columbian Magazine* of April 1788. The second "genius" he celebrated was William Billings, a Boston musician whose importance has increasingly been recognized in the twentieth century.[83] The first, however, was "the late *Robert Bolling,* Esq. of Chellow, in the county of Buckingham in Virginia." Du Ponceau extravagantly called him "one of the greatest poetical geniuses that ever existed." He stated that Bolling "has left behind him two volumes of poetry in the *Horatian* style, which I have read with the greatest delight and which, in my opinion, are worthy to be translated with honour to posterity."

Du Ponceau, a native of France, found it remarkable that Bolling "had acquired the Latin, French and Italian, so as to be able to write elegant poetry, in every one of those languages." Du Ponceau had made copies of several of Bolling's poems, but the only one he had not lost was "an Italian piece written by him, *on himself,* which, for the purity of style, and simplicity of composition, a *Metastasio* would not disown, and which I have sent, as a sample of his taste, to be inserted in your poetical department."[84] (Because the poem, "Notizia di Messer Roberto Bolling," is not contained in any of Bolling's extant manuscript volumes, we must assume that at least one volume examined by Du Ponceau at Chellow is not among those that have survived.)[85] Learning from Thomas Jefferson that Theodorick Bland, Jr., was Bolling's literary executor, Du Ponceau talked with Bland about Bolling. He concluded by "expressing the most ardent wish" that Bland "may soon give to the world those elegant monuments of American genius."[86] But Bland died in 1790, and except for occasional brief notices, Bolling remained comparatively unknown in American literature until 1969.[87]

THE JOURNAL IN AMERICAN LITERATURE

As literature, Robert Bolling's "Circumstantial Account" compares favorably with the best colonial American journals. As a genre, the journal is similar to the diary, for it is typically a diarylike account kept for a specific purpose or for a special period. The diary, of course, is simply a day-by-day record of activities, not kept for a specific occasion. The four classic journals of colonial America are *The Narrative of the Captivity and Restauration of Mrs. Mary Rowlandson,* her record of captivity in 1676 during King Philip's War; the *Journal* of Madame Sarah Kemble Knight, which she kept on a trip from Boston to New York and back in 1704–5; William Byrd's masterpiece, *The History of the Dividing Line,* a revision of the journal he kept while surveying the boundary between Virginia and North Carolina in 1729; and Dr. Alexander Hamilton's *Itinerarium,* his record of a trip in 1744 from Annapolis, Maryland, to Maine and back. To these four, we must now add Robert Bolling's "Circumstantial Account," the detailed narrative of his courtship of Anne Miller in 1760, written as a letter to a friend in England.[88]

Mary Rowlandson had the most dramatic subject matter.[89] Her captivity narrative begins with an Indian raid and the violent deaths of most of her friends and family. She described the incredible hardships she underwent as the Indians made one after another "remove" through fear of pursuit by the colonial militia; her blind contempt and hatred for the Indians as a group even while she learned which individuals among them could and would be kind and considerate to her; her increasing hunger and gradual toughening as she became inured to the life and fare of her Indian captors; her ceaseless searching for signs of God's approval and examination of her captivity experience as a symbolic version of her spiritual salvation; and her complete honesty and lack of self-consciousness, whether telling of such incidents as taking the food from the fingers of a child or relating that her Indian owner, returning after an absence of several weeks, was surprised at her filthiness, gave her a bit of mirror, and bade her go and wash herself. Her story is fascinating—the classic Indian captivity narrative and a brilliant, unself-conscious self-portrayal of a Puritan matron.

Sarah Kemble Knight's *Journal* is self-conscious, literary, ironic, and deliberately humorous.[90] Of course, she faced no great dangers—except her own fear of water, of being lost, and of traveling at night. Just as she was aware of the appearance that she—a middle-aged, plump, energetic, opinionated woman—made, so too she constantly judged the appearance and character of others. She was a social satirist, with an eye for character types and an appreciation for the motifs of American literature and society. She enjoyed oral anecdotes and recorded them with interest, for example, the origin of the word *Narragansett* or the story of two Connecticut justices at a pumpkin bench who were bested by an Indian's wit. Though Knight's journal was written less than forty years after Mary Rowlandson's, the two women reflected totally different external and internal worlds. The secular Madame Knight, unlike the scrupulously honest, solemn, religious, persevering, and tough Mary Rowlandson, was a businesswoman with an eye on the main chance, an ironic satirist, and a playful writer.

William Byrd began his *History of the Dividing Line* as a diary, revised it into a "Secret History" satirizing the foibles of the others (especially the North Carolinians) present on the trip, and again revised it (incorporating parts of the manuscript history of Virginia he had written more than thirty years before) into the *History*.[91] The style has all the polished wit and rhetoric of a Restoration play—and even (when the pioneers encounter a woman or when he can drag in a sexual allusion) something of its subject matter. Indirectly, Byrd dealt with topics of eighteenth-century intellectual interest. When the surveyors encountered a "hermit" at the beginning of their journey, Byrd satirized primitivism and, implicitly, the usual eighteenth-century condemnations of luxury. Conscious of his English audience, he wrote a guide to wilderness woodcraft, giving information about what kind of food to take along on extended trips into the wilderness. He displayed an appreciation for the "romantic" views (he used the word in an avant-garde way, revealing a keen literary sensitivity) of mountains and valleys in the wilderness and repeatedly revealed himself to be (what a satirist must be) a sharp observer of manners and of men. When he received a letter from home, he was conscious of an unusual tension among the party and observed that his friend William Dandridge took up a special position to watch him read it. It seems that the men had all heard that Byrd's only son was critically ill and was expected to die, but they had kept the news from him to spare him anxiety until the outcome was certain.[92] Dandridge was ready to comfort Byrd if the letter bore the anticipated dread news. (Fortunately, Byrd's son had recovered.) Byrd did not spell all this out, but his *History of the Dividing Line* is filled with such examples of keen sensitivity to the actions and psychology of others.

The fourth of the best-known colonial American journals is Dr. Alexander Hamilton's *Itinerarium*.[93] It is the best portrait of urban life and of traveling in colonial America that we have. Like William Byrd,

Hamilton was alert to the latest intellectual fashions, and he anticipated the Hudson River school of painters in his appreciation for the "wild, romantic" scenery found along that river. Like Madame Knight, he ironically appreciated his own appearance (complete with plumed hat, a brace of pistols in case he encountered highwaymen, and a slave to care for his portmanteau and baggage) and recorded with wry amusement the comments of others about him. He read the latest English literature and revealed his love for such past great writers as Spenser. Like Knight, he appreciated colonial culture and recorded its folk customs and anecdotes. His letters of introduction brought him into the society of the best-known colonial American intellectuals. Above all, Hamilton's journal is revealing for its portrayal of mid-eighteenth-century colonial urban life—the coffeehouses, taverns, club life, and great variety of colonial American characters.

Robert Bolling's journal must now be admitted into the company of these other colonial American journals. It contains our best record of love, courtship, jealousy, lust, and passion in colonial America. It is also one of the most revealing portraits of a colonial Virginian's pride—a distinguishing characteristic of the Virginia aristocracy, according to contemporaries and later observers. The "Circumstantial Account" has greater structure than most other journals of early America—most of which are merely travel diaries, with a beginning and ending that is the arbitrary result of the start and the finish of a trip. Only Mary Rowlandson's, among the classic journals of colonial America, has an equal sense of beginning and conclusion, but she is the least artful writer of the major diarists. (Her very lack of self-consciousness, in fact, is part of the excellence of her captivity narrative.) Bolling wrote with an art comparable to that of Knight, Byrd, and Hamilton.

He had, on occasion, the polished wit of William Byrd. "No one," said Bolling, "suffers more, or is less pitied than a discarded Lover." The journal builds up to a climax, and we find more circumstantial detail given in Bolling's descriptions of "the to me famous 16 of September" than in any preceding episode. At Hood's, on September 16, Anne Miller was "seated in a large Windsor Chair in the Piazza." The journal seemingly records the exact words of her conversation with Bolling. The setting and the walk in the garden are detailed precisely. Then James

Johnson intruded into the circumscribed space, a snake violating the garden as he lied to Anne Miller: "He insinuated to her, that Mr. Miller had personal Objections to me and that, for the ensuing two Years, we were to have no Manner of Communication whatever: both which Assertions were contrary to that Gentleman's repeated Declarations." The diction in this context—particularly the use of the word *insinuated* (the connotative implications of snakelike are at least as important as the denotative meaning of "to introduce gradually and insidiously")—is excellent. Altogether, Bolling's "Circumstantial Account" ranks with the most fascinating colonial American journals.

Three aspects of Bolling's courtship journal are unusual. First, every reader initially will be surprised at its literariness. It abounds with allusions to Italian, Latin, French, and English literature and contains Bolling's poems imitating Italian classics. Even at age twenty-two, Bolling was the foremost devotee of Italian literature in colonial America. He was saturated in literature and constantly saw his experiences paralleling situations in previous literature. He no doubt found the literary comparisons vaguely comforting, for they enabled him to distance himself from the painful experiences he had undergone. In Rowlandson's case, the providential view allowed her almost to escape the normal bounds of self-consciousness. Similarly, Bolling's literary lenses allowed him to put into perspective the raw emotions of love, anguish, disappointment, and frustration that fill the journal. At the same time, the allusions reassured Bolling that his experience was not abnormal or even terribly unusual. And further, Bolling's consciousness of past literatures containing comparable situations and emotions not only allowed him additional freedom to record his actions and to express his emotions but also made him view his personal experiences through literary lenses.

Few people of his time were so filled with the literary imagination. No other colonial American writer was. His contemporaries frequently were angered by Bolling's seeming obliviousness to their supposedly private feelings. But the increasingly genteel world of a middle class in the making, reflected so perfectly by the *Spectator* and *Tatler*, was not one of Petrarchan verse and anti-Petrarchan satire. In rejecting the amorous language and sentiments of Eliosa in Alexander Pope's "Eloisa to Abelard" in 1782, Lucinda Lee not only reflected the genteel world of the *Spectator* and *Tatler* but also dismissed the tradition of the Ovidian heroic epistle. Bolling was steeped in such literary traditions and, more than any other colonial American, viewed his experiences through them. His major poem of 1773, "A Copy of Verses in Praise of Winter," aroused a storm of protest from such other Virginia litterateurs as John Page and Robert Munford partially because they did not recognize that the long poem imitated an Italian classic.

A second unusual aspect of Bolling's courtship journal is that it was written after the events it describes. Most journals are diaries kept for a special time or purpose. Even Mary Rowlandson's captivity narrative seems to have been based upon notes that she kept at the time, though it was revised later. But Bolling's courtship journal evidently was written after Anne Miller sailed from Virginia on October 17, 1760. The whole account is therefore suffused with Bolling's bitter feelings about the outcome of the affair, though he occasionally forgot his resentment in reliving the courtship's happier moments. The "Appendix" seems to have been added several years after Anne Miller's return to Virginia and her marriage to Peyton Skipwith, for Bolling had forgotten the exact dates of those events, and he referred there to the death of his wife Mary Burton, which occurred on May 2, 1764. It appears, therefore, that the journal-epistle was written in the late fall of 1760 or the winter of 1760–61, and that the appendix was added sometime after 1766.

The third unusual aspect of Bolling's journal is its documentary nature. Because it was composed after the events took place, Bolling wanted to certify that the account was true—not just sour grapes on his part. His title, "A Circumstantial Account," stresses the objectivity and the detailed nature of the story that follows. The first document included in the journal, if we do not count the prefatory poems, is his map of the area where the courtship occurred. The map implies that what follows is as true as the physical reality of the area's geography. Further, a series of letters document the progress of the courtship. There are two letters by Robert Bolling to Anne Miller, one of February 27 and the other, recriminatory one of September 30. There are no less than four letters or snippets of letters from Bolling's friends and advocates: two from Jerman Baker, August 19 and 22; one from Bolling Starke of September 4; and one from Colonel Alexander Bolling of September 8. And finally, there is even a letter from Anne Miller to her father, August 26. All the documents testify, directly and indirectly, to the story's truth. In the future, Bolling's courtship journal will be recognized as a minor classic of colonial American literature.

NOTES

1. For colonial Virginia diaries and for journals kept by visitors to Virginia, see Jane Carson, *Travelers in Tidewater Virginia, 1700–1800: A Bibliography* (Charlottesville: University Press of Virginia, 1965).

2. Jane Carson, *Colonial Virginians at Play* (Williamsburg, Va.: Colonial Williamsburg Foundation, 1965), 23–35; Daniel Blake Smith, *Inside the Great House: Planter Family Life in Eighteenth-Century Chesapeake Society* (Ithaca, N.Y.: Cornell University Press, 1980), 135–40; Rhys Isaac, *The Transformation of Virginia, 1740–1790* (Chapel Hill: University of North Carolina Press, 1982), 80–87.

3. *The Revolutionary Journal of Baron Ludwig von Closen, 1780–1783*, tr. and ed. Evelyn M. Acomb (Chapel Hill: University of North Carolina Press, 1958), 176–77. See the similar comment by Jean-François-Louis, comte de Clermont-Crèvecoeur, in tr. and eds., Howard C. Rice, Jr., and Anne S. K. Brown, *The American Campaigns of Rochambeau's Army, 1780, 1781, 1782, 1783*, 2 vols. (Princeton, N.J.: Princeton University Press, 1972), 1:66.

4. Upon returning with the Carters from dancing, Philip Fithian wrote: "We got to Bed by three after a Day spent in constant Violent exercise" (*The Journal and Letters of Philip Vickers Fithian, 1773–1774: A Plantation Tutor of the Old Dominion*, ed. Hunter Dickinson Farish [1943; rpt. Williamsburg, Va.: Colonial Williamsburg, Inc., 1965], 155).

5. Ibid., 33; see also 47, 57.

6. Ibid., 19, 32, 33–34, 66, 123, 124, 125, 178, 241 n.29.

7. "Extracts from the Letter-Books of Lieutenant Enos Reeves, of the Pennsylvania Line," ed. John B. Reeves, *Pennsylvania Magazine of History and Biography* 21 (1897–98): 381. The ball took place on January 31, 1782, at the home of Colonel Thomas Eaton of Granville, N.C. His father came to North Carolina about 1739 from Petersburg, Va. Eaton's first wife, married c. 1761, was Anna Bland, Bolling's second half cousin, the sister of

Dr. Theodorick Bland (Bolling's literary executor). Eaton's second wife, married 1781, was another Virginian, Anne Stith (daughter of Buckner Stith), a descendant of the same Stith family that included Anne Stith, the second wife of Bolling's great-grandfather, Colonel Robert Bolling, the emigrant. For a sketch of Eaton, see *Dictionary of North Carolina Biography*, ed. William S. Powell (Chapel Hill: University of North Carolina Press, 1979—), 2:131.

8. Fithian (62) recorded two times when the elder Carter son, Ben (Benjamin Tasker Carter) and Robert Carter's nephew Harry (Henry Willis), danced with the blacks who were playing the banjo and a fiddle.

9. Andrew Burnaby, *Travels through North America*, ed. Rufus Rockwell Wilson (New York: A. Wessels Co., 1904), 26. Cresswell noted: "Betwixt the Country dances they have what I call everlasting jigs. A couple gets up and begins to dance a jig (to some Negro tune) others comes and cuts them out, and these dances always last as long as the Fiddler can play. This is sociable, but I think it looks more like a Bacchanalian dance than one in a polite assembly" (*The Journal of Nicholas Cresswell, 1774–1777* [New York: Dial Press, 1924], 53).

10. Quoted in Carson, *Colonial Virginians at Play*, 22n.

11. Richard Lewis, "Verses, To the Memory of His Exclly Benedict Leonard Calvert . . . ," in Walter B. Norris, "Some Recently Found Poems on the Calverts," *Maryland Historical Magazine* 32 (1937): 124.

12. "The Journal of Ebenezer Hazard in Virginia, 1777," ed. Fred Shelley, *Virginia Magazine of History and Biography* 62 (1954): 409; Robert Hunter, Jr., *Quebec to Carolina in 1785–1786*, ed. Louis B. Wright and Marion Tinling (San Marino, Calif.: Huntington Library, 1943), 207; *The American Journals of Lt. John Enys*, ed. Elizabeth Cometti (Syracuse, N.Y.: Syracuse University Press, 1976), 218.

13. *Maryland Gazette*, Aug. 21, 1760, p. 2. One contestant died immediately after the fight. Allan Kulikoff identifies the two as tenant farmers (*Tobacco and Slaves: The Development of Southern Cultures in the Chesapeake, 1680–1800* [Chapel Hill: University of North Carolina Press, 1986], 228–29).

14. *The Diary of Samuel Sewall*, ed. M. Halsey Thomas, 2 vols. (New York: Farrar, Straus and Giroux, 1973), 2:960.

15. Smith, *Inside the Great House*, 138. As more kinds of evidence are used and as more information becomes available, scholars increasingly note the dis-

crepancy between the facts of actual behavior and the proprieties as expressed both in the etiquette books and the more genteel literature with the facts of actual behavior. See Roger Thompson, *Sex in Middlesex: Popular Mores in a Massachusetts County, 1649–1699* (Amherst: University of Massachusetts Press, 1986), esp. chap. 2, "Courtship and Patriarchal Authority," pp. 34–53.

16. [Lucinda Lee Orr], *Journal of a Young Lady of Virginia* (Baltimore: John Murphy and Co., 1871), 49.

17. Edmund S. Morgan, *Virginians at Home: Family Life in the Eighteenth Century* (Williamsburg, Va.: Colonial Williamsburg Foundation, 1952), 36. Morgan's brief book on the subject has been superseded by the works cited in n. 2, as well as by Jan Lewis, *The Pursuit of Happiness: Family and Values in Jefferson's Virginia* (Cambridge: Cambridge University Press, 1983). Morgan wrote before the challenging work done by Philippe Ariès, *Centuries of Childhood: A Social History of Family Life*, tr. Robert Baldick (New York: Knopf, 1962); Edward Shorter, *The Making of the Modern Family* (New York: Basic Books, 1975); and Lawrence Stone, *Family, Sex, and Marriage in England, 1500–1700* (New York: Harper & Row, 1977). Daniel Blake Smith has surveyed the scholarly literature to 1981 in "The Study of the Family in Early America: Trends, Problems, and Prospects," *William and Mary Quarterly*, 3d ser., 39 (1982): 1–28.

18. The comte de Clermont-Crèvecoeur, in Rice and Brown, *American Campaigns of Rochambeau's Army*, 1:66; cf. 72 n.

19. Daniel Scott Smith and Michael S. Hindus proved that from 1749 to 1780 between one-fourth and one-third of all women in Kingston Parish, Gloucester County, Virginia, were pregnant when married ("Premarital Pregnancy in America, 1640–1971: An Overview and Interpretation," *Journal of Interdisciplinary History* 5 [1975]: 563).

20. Neil Larry Shumsky demonstrated that the permission of the parent was extremely important in the seventeenth century but found that during the eighteenth century, "parents interfered less and less in the selection of their children's mates" ("Parents, Children, and the Selection of Mates in Colonial Virginia," *Eighteenth-Century Life* 2 [1975]: 86).

21. Smith, *Inside the Great House*, 127–29.

22. Andrew Burnaby thought Virginians were "vain and imperious" and attributed their pride to their "authority over their slaves." He speculated, too, that "The public or political character of the Virginians corresponds with their private one: they are haughty and jealous of their liberties, impa-

tient of restraint, and can scarcely bear the thought of being controuled by any superior power" (*Travels*, 54, 55). See also "Journal of Josiah Quincy, Junior, 1773," *Proceedings of the Massachusetts Historical Society* 49 (1915– 16): 467; Fithian, *Journal*, 161.

23. *Benjamin Franklin: Writings*, ed. J. A. Leo Lemay (New York: Library of America, 1987), 1250.

24. *The Official Papers of Francis Fauquier, Lieutenant Governor of Virginia, 1758–1763*, ed. George Reese, 3 vols. (Charlottesville: University Press of Virginia, 1980–83), 1:326–420.

25. See John Seelye, *Prophetic Waters: The River in Early American Life and Literature* (New York: Oxford University Press, 1977), for inspired reflections on the importance of the river.

26. Robert Wheeler, "The County Court in Colonial Virginia," in *Town and County: Essays on the Structure of Local Government in the American Colonies*, ed. Bruce C. Daniels (Middletown, Conn.: Wesleyan University Press, 1978), 111–33. Wheeler begins with an overview of the county's significance in colonial Virginia.

27. *The Fry & Jefferson Map of Virginia and Maryland: Facsimiles of the 1754 and 1794 Printings with an Index* (Charlottesville: University Press of Virginia, 1966).

28. See "Cobbs" in the Glossary.

29. Churchill Gibson Chamberlayne, ed., *The Vestry Book and Register of Bristol Parish, Virginia, 1720–1789* (Richmond: C. G. Chamberlayne, 1898), 342. England and the American colonies used the Julian calendar (in which the new year began on March 25) until September 1752, when they adopted the Gregorian calendar. For dates before September 3, 1752, I follow the Old Style calendar but give both Old and New Style years for the period from January 1 to March 25.

30. Mildred K. Abraham, "The Library of Lady Jean Skipwith," *Virginia Magazine of History and Biography* 91 (1983): 296–347.

31. Philip Slaughter, *A History of Bristol Parish, Va.*, 2d ed. (Richmond: Randolph and English, 1879), 23–26. Slaughter only says that the author was "a great-great-grandson of the Princess Pocahontas," but the style and opinions are those of Bolling.

32. Charles Campbell, ed., *The Bland Papers*, 2 vols. (Petersburg, Va.: E. and J. C. Ruffin, 1840–43), 1:19–20.

33. Ibid., 1:xx, 20.

34. Ibid., 1:23–24.

35. *The Poems of St. George Tucker of Williamsburg, Virginia, 1752–1827*, ed. William S. Prince (New York: Vantage Press, 1977).

36. John Burke, *Burke's Peerage and Baronetage*, ed. Peter Townend (London: Burke's Peerage, 1970), 2459–60; Benjamin Robert Kesler, "The Skipwith Family in Colonial Virginia" (M.A. thesis, University of Virginia, 1938).

37. *The Prose Works of William Byrd of Westover*, ed. Louis B. Wright (Cambridge: Harvard University Press, 1966), 319.

38. Cynthia Miller Leonard, *The General Assembly of Virginia, July 30, 1619–Jan. 11, 1978: A Bicentennial Register of Members* (Richmond: Virginia State Library, 1978), xx for John Rolfe; 49, 50, 59, 62, and 64 for Robert Bolling, the emigrant; 65, 67, 69, 72 for John Bolling I (burgess from Henrico in the assemblies of 1710–12, 1712–14, 1718, and 1723–26); and 74, 79, 81, 83, 86 for John Bolling II (burgess from Henrico and then Chesterfield County in the assemblies of 1728–34, 1742–47, 1748–49, 1752–55, and 1756–58). Because Robert Bolling, the emigrant (1646–1709), came to Virginia in 1660, he seems to provide another example of Bernard Bailyn's thesis that the great families of colonial Virginia generally emigrated in the latter part of the seventeenth century and that previous Virginia society was unstable. However, the Bollings were proudest of their descent from Powhatan and Pocahontas; and Thomas Rolfe (son of Pocahontas and John Rolfe) was certainly part of the stable society of post-1622 Virginia (Bernard Bailyn, "Politics and Social Structure in Virginia," *Seventeenth-Century America: Essays in Colonial History*, ed. James Morton Smith [Chapel Hill: University of North Carolina Press, 1959], 90–115; cf. Jon Kukla, "Order and Chaos in Early America: Political and Social Stability in Pre-Restoration Virginia," *American Historical Review* 90 [1985]: 275–98.

39. John Bolling II was the surveyor of Prince George County; the day after his death, Richard Bland wrote to Dr. Thomas Dawson that "Mr. Currie desires to be Surveyor of Prince George County, in place of Col. Bolling deceased" (Manuscript Collection, New York Public Library, Emmet 1058).

40. William Stith, *The History of the First Discovery and Settlement of Virginia* (Williamsburg, Va.: W. Parks, 1747), 146; Wyndham Robertson, *Pocahontas alias Matoaka, and Her Descendants*, ed. R. A. Brock (1887; rpt. Baltimore: Genealogical Publishing Co., 1968), 32–35.

41. William G. Stanard, "The Ancestors and Descendants of John Rolfe with Notices of Some Connected Families," *Virginia Magazine of History and Biography* 22 (1914): 331; Robert Bolling, *A Memoir of a Portion of the Bolling Family in England and Virginia*, tr. John Robertson, Jr., ed. T[homas] H. W[ynne] (Richmond: W. H. Wade & Co., 1868), 7.

42. Unless otherwise noted, all information concerning Bolling's early life is from his *Memoir*, 5–10. The date of his birth in the *Memoir*, 5, is New Style; in "Hilarodiana" (microfilm, University of Virginia Library), 21, Bolling said he was born at Varina, Aug. 17, 1738, "O.S."

43. Matthew Henry Peacock, *History of the Free School of Queen Elizabeth at Wakefield* (Wakefield: W. H. Milnes, 1892), 136–41; *DNB*, s.v. "Clarke, John."

44. William Beverley, "Diary of William Beverley of 'Blandfield' during a Visit to England," *Virginia Magazine of History and Biography* 36 (1928): 27–35, 161–69; Rind's *Virginia Gazette*, March 4, 1773, p. 2, col. 3; Bolling, "La Gazzetta . . ." (manuscript volume, Huntington Library, San Marino, Calif., acc. no. BR 73), 139 (draft) and 153.

45. Peacock, 169–70; Lucille Griffith, "English Education for Virginia Youth: Some Eighteenth-Century Ambler Family Letters," *Virginia Magazine of History and Biography* 69 (1961): 7–27. Although the Amblers and Lees attended the Heath Academy, the references within the letters prove that some of the boys transferred to the Wakefield school. Cf. Richard Beale Davis, *Intellectual Life in the Colonial South, 1585–1763*, 3 vols. (Knoxville: University of Tennessee Press, 1978), 1:357–58.

46. Bolling, *Memoir*, 10.

47. *Another Secret Diary of William Byrd of Westover, 1739–1741, with Letters and Literary Exercises, 1696–1726*, ed. Maude H. Woodfin, tr. Marion Tinling (Richmond: Dietz Press, 1941), 287.

48. Bolling, *Memoir*, 4; and "The Blunt Reply," in "Hilarodiana," 20. See the discussion and notes in J. A. Leo Lemay, "Robert Beverley's *History and Present State of Virginia* and the Emerging American Political Ideology," in *American Letters and the Historical Consciousness: Essays in Honor of Lewis P. Simpson*, ed. J. Gerald Kennedy and Daniel Mark Fogel (Baton Rouge: Louisiana State University Press, 1987), 84–86.

49. "Letter of Col. John Banister, of Petersburg, to Robert Bolling," *William and Mary Quarterly*, 1st ser., 10 (1901–2): 102–5; John A. Schutz, ed.,

"A Private Report of General Braddock's Defeat," *Pennsylvania Magazine of History and Biography* 79 (1955): 374–77.

50. E. Alfred Jones, *American Members of the Inns of Court* (London: St. Catherine Press, 1924), 23.

51. Griffith, 20.

52. Bolling, "Hilarodiana," 21.

53. Although Bolling, *Memoir*, 6, gave the date of his father's death as Sept. 6, John Randolph of Roanoke, copying a *Virginia Gazette* news notice (no longer extant), gave the date as Sept. 5 (*Virginia Magazine of History and Biography* 16 [1908]: 208). Richard Bland, writing to Dr. Thomas Dawson on Sept. 6, referred to John Bolling II as "deceased" (Manuscript Collection, New York Public Library, Emmet 1058). Perhaps he died about midnight.

54. John Randolph of Roanoke copied a notice of the marriage from the *Virginia Gazette* of Dec. 21, 1759 (no longer extant), into his "Commonplace Book," c. 1826, p. 11, Virginia Historical Society, Richmond (Gerald Steffens Cowden, "The Randolphs of Turkey Island: A Prosopography of the First Three Generations, 1650–1806" [Ph.D. diss., College of William and Mary, 1977], 183 n. 156).

55. Bolling, *Memoir*, 6–7.

56. J. A. Leo Lemay, *A Calendar of the American Poetry in the Colonial Newspapers and Magazines and in the Major English Magazines through 1765* (Worcester, Mass.: American Antiquarian Society, 1972), no. 1561.

57. I first identified Bolling as a prolific colonial Virginia poet and writer in *Proceedings of the American Antiquarian Society* 79 (1969): 303 (reprinted in my *Calendar*, xxii). I did not include almanacs in the *Calendar*. Bolling evidently wrote "The Lawyer and His Client, from Boileau Imitated" in the *Virginia Almanac . . . for . . . 1761* (Williamsburg, Va.: Hunter, 1760), Evans no. 8610.

58. William Waller Hening, ed., *The Statutes at Large: Being a Collection of All the Laws of Virginia . . .* 13 vols. (New York, Philadelphia, and Richmond: various publishers, 1819–23), 7:419–23.

59. *Journals of the House of Burgesses of Virginia, 1761–1765*, ed. John Pendleton Kennedy (Richmond: Virginia State Library, 1907), 3, 5, 33, 45, 63, 69, 169(?), 201, 225(?), 313, 327.

60. Stratton Nottingham, comp., *The Marriage License Bonds of Northampton County, Virginia, from 1706 to 1854* (1929; rpt. Baltimore: Genealogical Publishing Co., 1974), 9.

61. J. A. Leo Lemay, "Southern Colonial Grotesque: Robert Bolling's 'Neanthe,'" *Mississippi Quarterly* 35 (1982): 97–126.

62. Carl R. Dolmetsch printed Bolling's "Anecdote Relating to the Careless Husband" in "William Byrd II: Comic Dramatist," *Early American Literature* 6, no. 1 (1971): 18–19.

63. *London Magazine* 33 (Aug. 1764): 417. A manuscript copy is found in Bolling's "A Collection of Diverting Anecdotes, Bon-Mots, and Other Trifling Pieces, 1764" (manuscript volume, Huntington Library, San Marino, Calif., acc. no. BR 163), 1. Bolling noted that it was "Printed in the London Mag: afterwards in the Virg. Gazette for Nov: 16.1764." The version in the *London Magazine* was expanded to contain an unfavorable anecdote of the late seventeenth-century Virginia governor Lord Howard of Effingham (*Georgia Gazette*, May 23, 1765, p. 2, col. 1). Anonymous, *Funny Stories, or, The American Jester* (Worcester, Mass.: I. Thomas, 1795), 47–48, Evans no. 28720; *The Booker T. Washington Papers*, vol. 1, *The Autobiographical Writings*, ed. Louis R. Harlan and John W. Blassingame (Urbana: University of Illinois Press, 1972), 267–68.

64. Herbert R. McIlwaine, "Justices of the Peace of Colonial Virginia [1757–1775]," *Bulletin of the Virginia State Library* 14 (1921): 64, 77, 113, 127; *Executive Journals of the Council of Colonial Virginia*, ed. H. R. McIlwaine and Benjamin Hillman, 6 vols. (Richmond: State Library, 1925–66), 6:449.

65. Edythe Rucker Whitley, *Genealogical Records of Buckingham Co., Virginia* (Baltimore: Genealogical Publishing Co., 1984), 1.

66. William Montgomery Sweeny, ed., *Marriage Bonds and Other Marriage Records of Amherst County, Va., 1763–1800* (Lynchburg, Va.: J. P. Bell Co., 1937), 10.

67. The *Richmond Argus* for April 9, 1803, p. 3, reported his death.

68. A diary by Leneaus Bolling for January–March 1814 survives at the University of Virginia Library. Wyndham Robertson, 35, and Stanard, "Rolfe," 332, list Robert Bolling's children. On his travels through Virginia, Benjamin Henry Latrobe stayed at Captain William Murray's, where on May 10, 1796, he compiled a genealogy of the descendants of Pocahontas.

William Murray (1752–1815) was a first cousin of Bolling's. Murray's wife, Rebecca, was the daughter of Thomas Bolling, the poet's elder brother. She was the first cousin once removed of her husband William Murray. Because William Murray's mother, Anne Bolling Murray (c. 1715–1800), the youngest daughter of John Bolling I (1676–1729), was alive and well, she may have been Latrobe's primary informant (*The Virginia Journals of Benjamin Henry Latrobe*, ed. Edward C. Carter II et al. [New Haven: Yale University Press, 1977], 1:111–12). A recent excellent genealogy is Stuart E. Brown, Jr., Lorraine F. Myers, and Eileen M. Chappel, *Pocahontas' Descendants* (Berryville, Va.: The Pocahontas Foundation, 1985), where Bolling may be found on p. 39, no. 13; and his children on p. 39, no. 131; p. 40, no. 132; p. 50, no. 133; p. 59, no. 134; and p. 61, no. 135.

69. The *Maryland Gazette*, Oct. 30, 1766, printed a detailed account of the charge and trial. See also Isaiah Thomas, *The History of Printing in America*, ed. Marcus A. McCorison (New York: Weathervane Books, 1970), 557.

70. J. A. Leo Lemay, "Robert Bolling and the Bailment of Colonel Chiswell," *Early American Literature* 6 (1971): 99–142, esp. 142, n. to line 141.

71. See A. R. Riggs, "Penman of the Revolution: A Case for Arthur Lee," in *Essays in Early Virginia Literature Honoring Richard Beale Davis*, ed. J. A. Leo Lemay (New York: Burt Franklin & Co., 1977), 203–19.

72. Bolling's contemporary reputation can be gauged from a letter that his cousin Robert Pleasants, a member of the Society of Friends, wrote him on January 10, 1775, concerning the plight of "the poor Slaves." Pleasants said that they "have an equal right to freedom with ourselves; I think such a noble cause would not disgrace the sentiments & pen of a Bolling seriously to engage in it" (Huntington Library, San Marino, Calif., Brock Collection, box 12).

73. Jonathan Boucher, *Reminiscences of an American Loyalist* (Boston: Houghton Mifflin, 1925), p. 111; Lemay, "Bailment," esp. 124 n. 24; Lemay, review of Anne Y. Zimmer, *Jonathan Boucher, Loyalist in Exile*, in *Virginia Magazine of History and Biography* 87 (1979): 108–9.

74. Edward Dumbauld, *Thomas Jefferson and the Law* (Norman: University of Oklahoma Press, 1978), 94–120. See also Frank L. Dewey, *Thomas Jefferson, Lawyer* (Charlottesville: University Press of Virginia, 1986). Dewey (24) says that the name of the arbitrator is unknown, but on p. 137 he notes, "The case was presented to an arbitrator, Benjamin Waller, in writing." Dewey also comments that "Jefferson's records do not tell us who won the

argument, but since Jefferson charged £5 and Robert Bolling paid him twice that amount, it seems likely that Jefferson's client prevailed" (24). But Bolling paid the extra £5 for a copy of the arguments in the long case. The payment was not (as Dewey assumes on pp. 86–87) a gratuity. Bolling paid Jefferson on September 13, 1771. Dewey (87) says that the case was still on the chancery docket of the General Court in October 1772.

75. Bolling's surviving manuscript volumes include "Pieces concerning Vineyards & Their Establishment in Virginia," dated "Chellow, Buckingham co., 1773," Huntington Library, San Marino, Calif., acc. no. BR 64.

76. *A Collection of Plays and Poems, by the Late Col. Robert Munford*, ed. William Munford (Petersburg, Va.: W. Prentis, 1798), 199–203, Evans no. 34158; Jon Charles Miller, "*A Collection of Plays and Poems* . . . : A Critical Edition" (Ph.D. diss., University of North Carolina, Chapel Hill, 1979). Munford's "Answer to the 'Winter Piece'" is in Miller, 140–44, with notes at 224–29 and Bolling's original poem quoted at 273–78.

77. Buckingham County Tax Lists, acc. no. 20238, Virginia State Library and Archives, Richmond. The list published in Whitley, 10, begins "William Shaw, Peter Roy, John Asher, Jacob Cooper." I believe that the first three were white and that Jacob Cooper was given a full name to distinguish him from the other slave named Jacob.

78. The best collection of ballads concerning the battle is in Reuben Gold Thwaites and Louise Phelps Kellogg, eds., *Documentary History of Dunmore's War, 1774* (Madison: Wisconsin Historical Society, 1905), 361–62, 433–39.

79. *Revolutionary Virginia: The Road to Independence*, ed. William J. Van Schreeven, Robert L. Scribner, and Brent Tarter, 7 vols. (Charlottesville: University Press of Virginia, 1973–83), 3:307.

80. *The Papers of Thomas Jefferson*, ed. Julian Boyd et al. (Princeton, N.J.: Princeton University Press, 1951–), 1:238.

81. Pages of the Vestrybook of Tillotson Parish, Buckingham County, for April 3, 1771–March 31, 1774, Johns Memorial Church, St.-Patrick-with Wilmer Parish, Farmville, Va., and a transcription, Manuscripts Department, University of Virginia Library, acc. no. 9967. Bolling's "The Jaybird & Peahen: A Fable" ("A Collection," 58–64) attacks the Reverend William Peasley. Bolling mentioned him unfavorable several times in his writings.

82. Du Ponceau's account of his visit to Chellow, on June 1, 1781 (written as a

letter to his daughter on Sept. 15, 1837), contains many of the same sentiments, expressed in the same words, as "Observator's" account of Bolling
(see "The Autobiography of Peter Stephen Du Ponceau," ed. James L.
Whitehead, *Pennsylvania Magazine of History and Biography* 63 [1939]:
321–22).

83. David P. McKay and Richard Crawford, *William Billings of Boston: 18th
Century Composer* (Princeton, N.J.: Princeton University Press, 1975);
Hans Nathan, *William Billings: Data and Documents* (Detroit: Information
Coordinators for the College Music Society, 1976).

84. "Observator" [Pierre Etienne Du Ponceau], "An Account of Two Americans
of Extraordinary Genius in Poetry and Music," *Columbian Magazine* 2
(April 1788): 211–13. The poem, "Notizia di Messer Roberto Bolling,"
appeared in the poetry section of the same issue, p. 230.

85. Du Ponceau said that he wrote a tribute to Bolling in one of the volumes he
examined at Chellow on June 1, 1781 ("Autobiography," 321), but that
tribute is not in any of the known volumes of Bolling's verse. In addition to
the several volumes of Bolling's verse listed in the bibliography, I have
found references to four manuscript volumes of poetry that are not known
to survive: "Thalia" (two references in "La Gazzetta," 92, 137); "Mush-
rooms," 2 vols. (four references in "La Gazzetta," 21, 24, 116 [2]);
"Liverpool" (one reference in "La Gazzetta," 62); and "Hippocrene" (one
reference in "Hilarodiana," 12, one reference in "A Collection," 64, and
two references in "La Gazzetta," 113, 127). The references make it clear
that these four volumes are all of later date in Bolling's life than the extant ones.

86. Perhaps Bland sent in "Time's Address to the Ladies" to Matthew Carey's
American Museum, where it appeared in vol. 7 (January-June 1790), Appendix, pp. 30–31. The poem had earlier been published in the *London
Magazine* 33 (Jan. 1764): 45 (Lemay, *Calendar*, no. 1952), and a copy
exists in "La Gazzetta," 17–19.

87. In the *Proceedings of the American Antiquarian Society* 79 (1969): 303, I
pointed out that Bolling was "the most productive poet of mid-eighteenth-
century America," identified thirty-five of his poems in English magazines
before 1766, and noted that he was "America's foremost satirical and occasional poet of the 1760's, replacing Joseph Green as America's primary
practitioner of these dominant eighteenth-century genres" (reprinted in
Lemay, *Calendar*, xxii).

88. For an introduction to the diaries and journals of early America, see Steven E.

Kagle, *American Diary Literature, 1620–1799* (Boston: Twayne, 1979), though Kagle omits captivity narratives, including Mary Rowlandson's.

89. Many editions of her captivity narrative are available. The best is Robert K. Diebold, "A Critical Edition of Mrs. Mary Rowlandson's Captivity Narrative" (Ph.D. diss., Yale University, 1972; available from University Microfilms, Ann Arbor, Mich., order no. 72-29,535).

90. The standard edition of *The Journal of Madam Knight* was edited in 1920 by George Parker Winship (rpt. New York: Peter Smith, 1935).

91. See Byrd, *Prose Works*.

92. In maintaining that Byrd did not deeply love his own family, Michael Zuckerman omits this key evidence, which directly contradicts his thesis ("William Byrd's Family," *Perspectives in American History* 12 [1979]: 253–311). Although Kenneth A. Lockridge also does not cite this passage, he thoroughly refutes Zuckerman in *The Diary, and Life, of William Byrd II of Virginia, 1674–1744* (Chapel Hill: University of North Carolina Press, 1987), esp. 57–58.

93. *Gentleman's Progress: The Itinerarium of Dr. Alexander Hamilton*, ed. Carl Bridenbaugh (Chapel Hill: University of North Carolina Press, 1948); see also Robert Micklus, "The Delightful Instruction of Dr. Alexander Hamilton's *Itinerarium*," *American Literature* 60 (1988): 359–84.

Robert Bolling's Courtship Journal

.

Non é Duol cosi acerbo e cosi grave,
Che mitigato alfin non sia dal Tempo,
Consolator degli Animi dolenti,
Medicina ed Oblio di tutti i Mali.

Tasso nel Torisimondo [1]

CANZONETTA DI CHIABRERA.[2]

Stella's waving Hair flows down
In a Curl, not fair, but brown.
Blooming is her Cheek and shews
All the Beauties of a Rose
And her Lips beyond compare,   5
Deeper than Vermilion are.
Yet, since first I saw all This,
I've not had a Moment's Peace.
Lord! when first I felt the Smart
Of that Urchin in my Heart,   10
Every where I heard em say,
He did nothing but in Play,
That he would not, (no, not he,)
Hurt the Finger of—a Flea:
That from Venus he was born: —   15
Horrid Falsehood, I'll be sworn!
Never Goddess born was he;
But engendered by the Sea
On a Rock, a Tempest tore:
From its Roots and drove ashore.   20
There he learn'd, among the Waves,
How to torture us like Slaves!
True indeed, he sports and plays,
Has the prettiest little Ways,
Harmless, infantine his Air;   25
But, for God's Sake! Lads, beware!
Sporting, playing—I protest,
We've no longer Heart in Breast.
See how full of Rage and Spite!
Let him rave—but I will write.   30
Little Viper, Dragon, Fiend!

Why, Peacebreaker, shou'd I end?
Well thou knowest all the Pain
Every Moment I sustain;
And, by *thee* o'erwhelmed with Woe,   35
Wou'dst thou have me PRAISE thee too?

Textual Note
18   engendered]   engengered

A

Circumstantial Account
of Certain Transactions,
that once
greatly interested the Writer and which
terminated at Flower-de-Hundred, on
the sixteenth of September, 1760, as such juvenile
Transactions do frequently to the Satisfaction of Nobody.

Tout le Monde connait leur Imperfection,
Ce n'est qu' Extravagance et qu' Indiscretion:
Leur Esprit est mechant, et leur Ame fragile.
Il n'est rien de plus faible et de plus imbecille,
Rien de plus infidele; et, malgrè tout cela,
Dans le Monde on fait tout pour ces Animaux-lá.

Ecole des Femmes.[3]

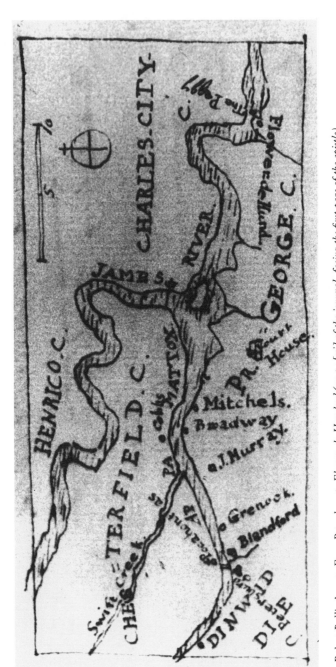

Robert Bolling's map: From Petersburg to Flower-de-Hundred (on p. [vi] of the journal, facing the first page of the epistle)

To R[obert?] B[everley?] Esq. in London.
Sir,

—Varium et mutabile semper Femina.

Virg.[4]

In my Neighbourhood, in Virginia, lived a Scotch Gentleman, whose Name was [Hugh] Miller. He always bore the Character of a Man of great Probity and strict Honor; tho, as to his religious Principles, which is indeed a Matter altogether foreign to our Purpose, he was a professed free-Thinker. He often, during the Life-Time of his Wife [Jane Miller], a Relation of mine, expressed an Inclination to return to his own Country; but, on her Decease, which happened in 1756, he absolutely determined. His eldest Daughter [Anne ("Nancy") Miller], who is to be the principal Subject of the ensuing Narrative, was then about fifteen Years old.

She was of a Disposition something uncommon. A certain *Impetus*, a Sprightliness in every Thought and Action, gave me the first Impressions in her Favor. But this Disposition had its Disadvantages, as that *Vis Animi* was no less visible in her Resentments than in her Pleasures and Attachments. Her Person was genteel and the Turn of her Face agreeable, tho not beautiful. She had a Haughtiness, I may even say, a Fierceness in her Countenance; which, on any little Emotion, destroyed, in some Degree, that pretty Softness, which is so amiable in a young Lady. With this Violence of Temper she had a Fund of good Sense, which served as a Counterpoise to that Defect: and which, as she grew older, seemed intirely to have mastered it.

It was not 'til the Year 1759 that I began to feel a particular Pleasure in this young Creature's Company. I knew the Obstinacy of her Father, and his positive Resolution to carry her with him to Great-Britain: and therefore confined myself, as much as possible, within the Bounds of Friendship: but the great Intimacy, between Relations in this Colony, permitting many Freedoms; I found it impossible to have this Lady in my Arms for Hours together, without feeling such Emotions, as are the unavoidable Consequence of much Familiarity between the Sexes. The pleasing Passion insensibly wrought itself into my Constitution, and became as much a Necessity with me as Hunger, Thirst, or any other involuntary Inclination. I therefore endeavoured, without making my Design public, to insinuate myself into her good Graces; and very often pressed her to declare what Hopes I might entertain. She gave no other than evasive Answers, expressing Doubts of my Sincerity and Apprehensions of her Father's Disapprobation. Nothing cou'd be more encouraging than this Kind of Behaviour. My Hopes were no wise diminished by an Accident, which discovered, I thought, that her Sentiments were not unfavorable.

A young Gentleman, on going to Grenock, the Place of her Abode, told her, he had just left me; and added, that, "was I not apprehensive, the World wou'd imagine me a Lover, I had waited on her myself." What, says she, and wept immoderately, does Mr. Bob Bolling think it a Disgrace, that the World shou'd believe, he loved me? Mrs. [Mary] Stark, who was present, and from whom I had this Relation, asked her, with some Surprize, whether I had ever made my Addresses to her. She replied—He is the properest Person to apply to: ask him. As no body knew, that this was real[l]y the Case, every one made his own Remark, and the Mistery was not cleared up 'till the Beginning of the Year 1760 ([Saturday] 12 January).

Miss Miller (being then at Badwington, the Seat [of] Robert Bolling, Esq., with several of her Relations, who were going, the next Day, to visit some Friends on Sappony River) I had the Imprudence, contrary to my usual Method, to intoxicate myself betimes. 'Twas on this Occasion that, forgetting every Thing, I gave Way to the Impulses of my Passion. I seized the dear Creature to my Bosom, kissed her a thousand Times, swore she was the sweetest little D——l on Earth, and, tho I hated Matrimony worse than Perdition; yet with her I wou'd not only submit to it with Pleasure, but even with Rapture. The Company was amazed, the Fair-one confounded, but not displeased. This rendered public an Affair, which ought first to have been perfected: however, to put the best Face on the Matter, I declared, that such were my real Sentiments: and informed Mr. Miller, by Message, of my Intentions. Some People censured me for not acquainting him with it myself; but, as that cou'd not have been done without quitting his Daughter, I shall, by the good-natured *Few*, be readily excused.

The Company went, the next day [Sunday, Jan. 13], to Bolling Starks, as was proposed: and on [Monday] the 14th to Bob Walker's, who had prepared an Entertainment. Miss Miller was my Partner. I never in my Life passed Time more to my Satisfaction. Every Part of my Nancy's Behaviour to me was as I cou'd wish it: and she publicly declared, that, of all Mankind, she chose me for her next Admirer. The Sun arose on our Mirth. My Transports were so great, that I scarce felt any of that Lassitude, which generally attends long Watching and great Exercise; but returned [on Tuesday, Jan. 15] with my Charmer to Mr. B[olling] Stark's, with all the Joy of a Bridegroom; for such, I doubted not, I shou'd be very shortly. Many of the Company congratulated me, as if my Success was a Thing certain: and nothing, during that Day, gave me the least Alarm. The *next* ([Wednesday, Jan.] 16) did by no Means answer my Expectations. My Nancy was silent when I put the Question; yet that Silence was no Consent—and—it was a Consent, that I expected. Indeed her good old Aunt Stark took some Pains to prevent my giving myself further Trouble; alleging, that she was well acquainted with my Mistress's Intentions, and that it wou'd be to no Purpose. This threw me into no small Amazement and seemed one entire Piece of Inconsistency. I therefore cou'd not follow her Advice, and ([Thursday] the 17), at Herbert Haynes's, I had an Opportunity of being better informed. I took Miss Miller a part and intreated, she wou'd tell me Whether her Friends and Country had not sufficient Charms to detain her *here*, and whether I might be the happy Person, she wou'd make Choice of, to accomplish that good End. She replied, with a Turn of Expression as little mortifying as possible, "That, if her Father left the Colony, she must in Duty wait on him." "May I hope, my dear Nancy, that you will return with me, if I follow you to Great-Britain?" "'Tis impossible for me to tell what may *then* be my Sentiments." "Tell me, I beseech you, Madam, what wou'd be your Sentiments, was it not for that Circumstance of your Father's Departure, and I shall readily guess what they will be hereafter?" "I hope, Sir, you will not think an Answer to that Question necessary." Somebody very opportunely led her out to dance and she left me in a Situation not to be described.

As no one suffers more, or is less pitied than a discarded Lover, I returned the next day [Friday, Jan. 18] from Sappony and did not see Miss Miller 'til [Thursday, Jan.] the 24, when, on my Entrance into the House at Broadway, I was not only surprized but somewhat diverted to observe her elevated on a Chest, in a Corner of the Room, with a Countenance, the most solemn I ever beheld.

It was by no Means my Design, that the Intimacy, which before subsisted between us, shou'd be dissolved; I therefore reproached her, for wearing that Air of Coldness, which, selon moi,[5] was by no Means deserved. She answered in such a Manner as to persuade me, it was rather Affliction than Contempt. Miss Miller, Miss [Elizabeth ("Betsy")] Stark, Benson Fieron and myself amused ourselves together, till 3 o'Clock: the greatest Part of which Time my Nancy passed immediately with me. I saw no Traces of that Reserve, with which Persons, in our Situation, generally treat each other.

Some Time after this I made a small Experiment. Carter Harrison had been one of our Company at Sappony, and was there discarded by Betsy Stark. He however continued his Addresses and was at Broadway ([Thursday, Jan.] 31) as was N[ancy] Miller. Carter's Mistress treated him with Complaisance, but, with Regard to myself, she was all Fondness. This, being a Kind of Behaviour not very usual with her, convinced me, her Design was to Alarm his Jealousy: a very proper Opportunity, I tho't, to enflame my own Charmer's. We had each the Success proposed. Carter seemed at the Gates of Death: the Agitation of Nancy Miller sufficiently envinced, that, if she had but little Esteem for me, she had at least a Quantity of self-Love, that cou'd ill-brook the Loss of an Admirer. At Sun-set my Sister [Mary Bolling] and a young Lady, who was with her, took Leave. Carter, his Mistress [Elizabeth Starke] and Miss Miller waited on us to the River. After the usual Salutations I was surprized to see the last-mentioned Lady (instead of going up the Hill with her Companions) seat herself on the River-Bank. Our Boat was going to put off, when I leaped on Shore and, without much Violence, brought her on Board. The young Ladies passed the greatest Part of that Night in my Chamber [at Cobbs]: but, as my Nancy was generally on a Bed with me, I had sufficient Opportunity to represent the Violence of my Passion and intreat a more favorable Sentence. "How can you ask me, my Cousin, when you know I can't." This she said in a melting Accent, and, I believe, was much affected. I expressed Apprehensions of her Attachment to Peyton Skipwith; but she gave me repeated Assurances, that they were ill-founded.

As I was obliged to set out the next Day ([Friday] Feb. 1) for my Plantations in Albemarle (since Buckingham), it gave me Pleasure to observe my Nancy shew some small Marks of Regret at Parting. The first Time I saw her afterwards was at a Ball, made by herself and Betsy Stark, at Blandford, [Wednesday, Feb.] 13. I endeavoured, tho' to no Purpose, to effect some Change in her Resolutions. I was her Partner at a second Ball, ([Friday, Feb.] 22) and there she assured me, that, tho' she cou'd not comply with my Desires, yet no one was dearer to her than myself. The Company of this young Lady was too agreeable, not to make me regret the want of it, when she was absent; I therefore acquainted her with a Determination, I had made, to avoid her Presence altogether. She beg'd I wou'd make no such Resolution, and invited me the next Day to her Father's. This Invitation I declined for the Reason above mentioned. Sometime after this ([Tuesday, Feb.] 26) a little Entertainment was made at Cobbs, to which herself, her Father and Mr. James Johnson (a Gentleman of whom I shall have Occasion to speak hereafter) were invited. There was an End of my Determination. I did indeed endeavour to behave to her with Indifference; but, coming by Accident into a Chamber, where she was sitting, extremely pensive, on a *Bed:* I cou'd no longer withhold, but overcome by an Excess of Passion, I threw myself *thereon,* and pressed her to my Bosom, with a Rapture, which can scarce be conceived. She reproached me with (but my Answers convinced her, I had no) Coldness. While we were together on the Bed I overlaid and broke a Fan of hers: a Necklace too had already fallen a Sacrifice to my Caresses. I tho't it necessary to make some Return for these Things, and sent her a

Necklace and Solitaire, a Fan and some other Trifles by Jerman Baker, who, as the sequel will shew, was very much my Friend. These Things were accompanied with a Letter of which this is a Copy.

To Miss Miller &c.

I have made you, dear Miss Miller, the greatest Offer, that any Gentleman can make a Lady. It was unworthy of you, and refused. I hope the small one, I now make, will not meet with the same Destiny. It does not deserve it, as it is altogether a Debt and not a Present. À Dieu, my dearest Nancy. Be persuaded, that I shall ever think with Regret on those Circumstances (whatever they are) which deprive me of the Power of saying, I am your

Feb. 27. 1760.   Bolling.

These Presents were returned, to my very great Vexation, and Nancy was inoculated,[6] at Mr. Bairds in Blandford, during an Excursion, I made, into Glocester. I therefore refused to visit her, 'til Mr. Baker declared to me, that he verily believed so outrageous an Indifference might have ill Consequences in her Disorder. For this Reason I did at last pay her a Visit, ([Sunday] 27 April) and had all the Room in the World to be satisfied of the Truth of his Information. She assured me, and wiped her Eyes, that it was not in Consequence of her own Inclination, she had returned my Presents; that she had acted comformably to the Advice of Messrs. [Bolling?] Stark and Johnson, and, in short, that my Displeasure gave her the greatest Concern in the World. During this her Hand was locked in mine, and her whole Countenance shewed an Earnestness, an Expression, that I never saw equal'd. Miss Suky Brooks, her Father's House-keeper, added, that she had wept on perusing my Letter, and she (S[uky] B[rooks]) was satisfied, if our Union never was completed, that the Failure ought not to be attributed to Miss Miller. My Nancy never once interrupted the Prattler. I retired, persuaded, she spoke like an Oracle.

I visited the poor Girl, (for she was extremely maltreated by the Small Pox) every now and then; and once at her own particular Desire. Suky was commissioned to inform me, that Messrs. Miller and Johnson were gone to Flower de Hundred and wou'd not return before the Saturday following, which was near a Week: and that my Company wou'd be acceptable on Thursday. This Information surpriz'd me a little, as I never had avoided the Presence of those Gentlemen. A Fit of the intermitting Fever attacked me immediately on my Arrival at Dr. Jameson's ([Thursday] 22 May) and kept me in Bed the whole Day.[7] The [Friday] 23 [May] I took Leave of my Nancy and seriously designed it my last Visit, agreeable to that excellent Maxim, "fugendo vinces":[8] However, to quote another, "L'Homme propose et Dieu dispose"; tho, to tell the Truth, I believe the Almighty had little to do, with some Things, that happened afterwards.

Tis necessary, tho I shall do it in a cursory Manner, to say something of Miss Claiborne. This Lady was inoculated ([Monday] June 2d) at Ireland with a Brother of her's, two Brothers of mine and some others. She had a fine Shape, some Sense and more Beauty, with a great Share of what the French call Douceur.[9] I was on a Visit ([Friday, June] 6) to these *Invalides*, and found Miss Miller arrived before me. This gave me no Pleasure. A certain coolness in her Behaviour, when with her last at Dr. Jameson's, had piqued me a good Deal: and I determined, on that Occasion, to make her smart for it. I took great Pains to tickle her Bosom with that pleasant Passion Jealousy. Never was Creature more uneasy. I embraced her coldly, but Roxana with Transport. Miss Miller placed herself at different Times on every Seat in the Room; at length, hardly able to contain her Resentment, she threw herself on the bed, exclaiming, with a visible Mortification, *Such Scenes!* and soon after withdrew. I cou'd scarce avoid being pleased with so pretty a creature as Roxana. As I was sensible of Nancy's Resolution to go to Scotland with her Father, 'twas prudent to encourage the first Motions of a new Passion: but, having Suspicions of her (Roxana) being under Engagements to Abner Nash, I was determined to conclude nothing, 'till those Doubts shou'd be removed and my old *Sweet-Heart* out of the Colony. Things remained sometime in this Situation. I saw them both almost every Day at Ireland, and there laid, without knowing it, the Seeds of that Storm, which broke out afterwards.

On [Wednesday] the 16th of July was the Sale of Mr. Miller's Household-Furniture, and a remarkable Æra in my Life; as, to the Consequences of that Day's Transactions, I owe the most uneasy Moments, I ever endured. Messrs. Dalgleish, Milner and my self had been employed some Days in appraising the Effects of J. Herberts Estate at Herbert's Place. This being accomplished about Noon, ([July] 16) I went thence to Grenock. It was no difficult Matter to get a Tête à Tête with my Nancy; for, as every Body was employed either in purchasing, or seeing Things purchased, at Auction, we retired unobserved into the Room called the Nursery; where we were near two Hours together. She gave me the most obliging Assurances, that she would write to me often after her Arrival in Scotland, and that, if Things shou'd turn out so that she cou'd return to Virginia, she declared, she wou'd give me immediate Information thereof. The Tears ran plentifully down her Cheeks. I must own, that, on that tender Occasion, I cou'd not forbear mixing my own with her's; and shewing a Sensibility, of which I was ashamed. When we took Leave, we neither of us spoke; but our mutual Concern was observed by more than one Person.

A few Days after ([Friday, July] 18) I sent her a very short Epistle, by Way of Farewell. This I delivered into the Hands of Mr. Baker &, at the same Time, commissioned him to obtain some Determination from her, on which I might lay some Stress. He was to insinuate to her, that, if she departed this Colony, even with favorable Sentiments for me, it was the same in Effect (If I was ignorant of them) as if she had prohibited me any Hopes at all; He was moreover to make Use of such other Arguments, as his own Imagination suggested. [Thursday] The 24 July I departed from Cobbs and retired to Chello, with Design to remain there, 'till after her Departure. But, on [Sunday] the 24 August, I received two Letters from Mr. Baker, of which the following are Extracts.

August 19. 1760. # # # # # # # # # # # # I spent a Day with Sylvia (so he called M[iss] Miller) at Roger Atkinson's. I took the Sanction of a clear, cool Evening and led her into the Garden, where I brought a lovely Hue on her Countenance, by asking her, if her best Friends might not entertain an Hope of seeing her in Virginia again? # # # # As I thought the Subject laudable, I chose to come to the Point; and, to remove the little Glow, which such a Question occasioned, I told her for whom I was Advocate. My Frankness was fully returned: and I was treated with all the Confidence, an open Heart cou'd desire. Sylvia mentioned the Bars there were to her Happiness. She urged Dependance, and the Will of a Parent: but I had no great Difficulty, in persuading her, that her own Happiness was the first and most necessary Consideration: that it was necessary, you shou'd have something to live on: and, that your Affection deserved a suitable Return: and upon my solemn Assurance of an unshaken Constancy on your Side (which she was much inclined to believe) she declared, *That* no one had ever shared her Affection with you: and, tho her Father shou'd object to her Return to Virginia, she was determined to tell him, as soon as he shoud be once settled, that Mr. Bolling was the only Man in the World, that shou'd be her Partner for Life. This was a kind Assurance, but there still lay another Bar, the Method by which you were to be acquainted with her Inclination. Virgin Modesty made a Struggle on the Point of her Writing to you; however, as difficult Points require Perseverance, I stuck to it: and she agreed to give you Notice, whenever a Visit from you might be conducive to the Happiness of both: and shou'd her Father continue to object to it, while she was in his Power, she was determined to wait, til *she* only had a Negative, and then she wou'd bestow her Hand where her Heart had taken it's Abode. &c. &c.

August 22. 1760. # # # # # # # # # #
From some Talk I have had with Sylvia I have discovered, that she has a great Desire to see you, before she Sails. This is a Satisfaction, I imagine, you will hardly refuse her; as, besides the Pleasure you must feel at seeing her, after what has passed between her and me, you may have the same Assurance from herself, in as full a Manner as you can wish. &c. &c. &c. &c. &c. &c. &c. &c. &c.

These agreeable Orders were punctually obeyed and I returned ([Monday, Aug.] 25) in a Day and Part of the Night to Cobbs, which is about ninety Miles. The next Morning ([Tuesday, Aug.] 26) I went early to Broadway. The Family were at Breakfast. Never did Eyes behold a Person in such a Situation as my Nancy. At my first Appearance a deadly Paleness overspread her Countenance, and she had near fainted;

but this presently gave Place to the most lively Glow, and the prettiest Confusion imaginable. This afforded Matter of great Speculation to the old Lady of Broadway [Mrs. Mary Starke] &c. who knew Nothing of the Renewal of my Addresses. The Attention Mr. Baker shewed my Mistress, during my Absence in Albemarle, had given Rise to quite contrary Conjectures. Mrs. Stark gave me a long History of their Courtship, which I listened to with much Curiosity til the Table was removed. *Then* the Mistery began to disappear. I led the blushing Fair into the Parloir and, having seated her in an easy Chair, received the warmest Assurances of the most inviolable Constancy. The tender Overflowings of a long restrained Passion fell from her Eyes, and the dear Creature appeared lost in those Sentiments by which myself was absorbed. But when I proposed her writing to her Father, to obtain his Consent to her Continuance in this Country, how beautiful were the Struggles between her Fear of giving him Pain, And the Regard she had just professed for me! The latter however gained the Victory, and this is, Word for Word, what she wrote that Gentleman; it being copied from the Original which I have in my Hands.

[The following note is written sideways in the middle of the page, so that Anne Miller's letter occupies the entire next page.] Vide Miss Miller's Letter to her Father which for particular Reasons I show contain one intire Sheet. The old Lady at Broadway writ the Letter & Nancy Miller copied it. The old Creature rendered the Expression's as gross as possible I believe with Design.

> *To* Mr. Hugh Miller.
> Dear Daddy,   August 26. 1760.
>   Pray be so good as calmly to read this Letter; for, I must tell you, my whole Happiness depends on it. Not to keep my dear Daddy any longer in Suspense, I have fixed my Affections on Mr. Bolling; nor is it in my Power ever to be tolerably happy, unless you will be so good as to consent to my marrying him. He is no Stranger to my Inclinations: he wou'd have waited on you himself, but I made it my Choice to prepare you for a Visit from him on this Occasion. Do not believe, good Sir, that it is a sudden Thought: no: for some time I have prefer'd him to all Mankind; but did not think my Affections

were so deeply rooted, 'till I found we were to be separated forever: which, give me Leave to tell you, I believe, will be impossible. so must conclude your

dutiful Daughter
Ann Miller

> See from Stella's charming Eyes
> How the forked Light'ning flies:
> Arrows wound in every Glance,
> Every Look a Dagger plants;
> Yet such melting Graces join,   5
> Stung to Death, we scarce repine;
> For that Softness seems to cure
> All the Harm, they did before:
> Yet, in Truth, it doth not heal,
> Witness, Love: I suffer still.[10]   10

Suky Brooks was immediately dispatched exprès to deliver the above Epistle to Mr. Miller at Flower-de-Hundred. I remained with Miss Miller and received every Moment some little, endearing, tho' nameless Mark of the most ardent Affection.

Mr. Baker arrived in the Afternoon and greatly disapproved of what had been done. He insisted, that the Mine shoud not have been sprung, 'til Nancy Miller had attended her Father to Great-Britain: and, upon the whole, prognosticated no Good from the Measures that had been taken. Tho' I was in my own Mind of a quite different Opinion, yet these Reflections, to which my Nancy was not privy, rendered me extremely thoughtful; while that tender Creature endeavoured, by the sweetest Arguments in the World, to remove the Chagrin by which I was devoured, I mean, by Assurances of an unshaken Fidelity.

I waited, as was proposed, the next Day on Mr. Miller ([Wednesday, Aug.] 27). He treated me with a Civility, I by no Means expected; but which, I found afterwards, was occasioned by his Apprehension of our making an Elopement. He was however severe enough in his Determination, which was, that, If for two Years we continued to have the same Sentiments for each other, we then professed, he wou'd give his Consent to our Union; and added, that, if I cou'd accomodate my Circumstances, so as to live in Great-Britain, it wou'd lessen, if not intirely remove, his Objections. He declared he had none against myself in particular, but cou'd not bear the thoughts of a Separation from his Daughter, whom, he said, I might visit at his House 'till the two Years expired. I desired his Permission to be as much as possible with her, while she continued in Virginia. This he refused, at first; alleging, that it might transport us both to take Measures, that might not then even enter our Imaginations. When I insisted—Well, says he, you may, if you please, attend her down. This Reply I considered, tho' it seems it was not intended, as a Compliance with my Request.

Mr. Hood, in every Part of his Carriage to me, steadily adhered to the Character he had always born—of being a Gentleman of Humanity and Honor. Mr. James Johnson adhered as steadily to the *one*, he had always deserved, of being an artful, designing Scoundrel. I desired him, in Miss Miller's Name, not to deviate from that Friendship, he had always professed for her; but be Mediator between her and her Father, in promoting this Affair. He replied, that Nancy was as dear to him as one of his own Children. (He shou'd have said as his Wife) that she might be assured, he wou'd do every Thing, to promote her Happiness and that there was not *A Man in the whole Wurrld* he had rather shou'd be her Husband than myself. I take God to Witness, that this is the Substance, and almost verbatim, of what he said to me. But so far was this worthy Gentleman from performing his Promise, that the Disappointments, which afterwards happened, are attributed, by those who cou'd be best informed, solely to his Influence over Mr. Miller and false Representations to his Daughter. I, the same Evening, gave that Lady an Account of my Transactions, at Broadway.

The next Day ([Thursday, Aug.] 28) she went to Mitchels, where she scared me almost out of my Senses, and made me think myself one of the most ungenerous Rascals, that ever existed. In a very tender Tête à Tête, we had in the Parloir, I cou'd not help, on reflecting upon the Difficulties to be surmounted, expressing some Fears, that she wou'd not be equal to the Trial. She received this Declaration *comme un Coup de Foudre*.[11] The Tears streamed down her Face: she appeared quite inconsolable. Mrs. Stark just then entering the Room—"O Madam," said she to her, "I cannot persuade him to believe me," and sobbed and sighed abundantly. After using every Argument, that the most unfeigned Contrition cou'd furnish, and swearing, she kept me in Tortures, she was appeased and her Countenance resumed it's wonted Serenity. This Scene was acted several Times during her Abode at Mitchels.

—————————————In breve Spatio

S'adira, e in breve Spatio anco si placa

Femina, Cosa mobil per Natura

Piu che Fraschetta al Vento, e piu che Cima

Di pieghevole Spica.

L'Aminta de Tasso.[12]

I saw this affectionate Creature every Day. My whole Joy was in her company and that Pleasure appeared altogether reciprocal. On [Wednesday] the third of September she was informed, that the Departure of the Peggy was deferred: and, as she wanted Necessaries for herself and Sisters, Miss Suky was dispatched to F[lower] de H[undred] for a Supply. In the mean Time my Happiness at Mitchels began to culminate. I really was ([Thursday, Sept.] 4) in Extacies. My Charmer was charmed and that Circumstance redoubled my Felicity. It was on that happy Day (The last I spent in her Company, without having my Joys at least equalled by my Fears,) that she permitted me to measure, what is called, the wedding Finger. I accordingly ordered a Ring to be made, after that Measure, by Mr. Hare of Pocahontas. On my Return from that Place ([Friday, Sept.] 5) I found Miss Suky just arrived, but with very ill News, from F[lower] de H[undred]. She reported, that Mr. Miller was much displeased at my seeing his Daughter. Strange! that he shou'd imagine, I wou'd remain within two Miles of, and not make her one Visit. In Consequence of this, my Nancy, after weeping in the most affectionate Manner, concluded with desiring me not to give her Father that Subject of Uneasiness. I must own, that the Request not only surprized but displeased me. I apprehended, that, if Consensus et non Concubitus facit Matrimonium, as say the Civilians, she owed me more Duty, as her Husband,

•63•

than she did her Father.[13] I departed, without taking Leave. On my Return to Cobbs the following Letter was put into my Hands.

> Flower-de-Hundred.   Thursday 4, 7[Septem]ber[14] 1760
> Dear Bob,
>   Mr. Johnson's Pride prompts him strongly to exert his Influence over Mr. Miller to carry his Daughter with him; and consequently he is your Enemy: you may be assured he is. Strange, that a Man of Mr. Miller's Understanding shou'd not be capable of disposing his own Children! No Oratory or Arguments will work on Johnson. Mr. Miller is in a Situation, which renders any Application from your Friends to him, a Point too tender. The Assurances, he gave you, depend are sincere; and cou'd either your Mother's Reconciliation to your leaving her, or the Connection between Miller and Johnson be weakened, in this particular—it wou'd be a great Point gained: I fear both are impracticable.   &c.   &c.   &c.

My Absence from Colonel [Alexander] Bollings was three Days. During this Miss Miller was, according to all Appearance, the most miserable Creature alive, wished herself dead a thousand Times, and declared she wou'd give the whole World to see me return. I wrote ([Monday, Sept.] the 8th) to Col. Bolling, requesting his Advice on the Occasion; and to know whether he thought it convenient for me to repair to Mr. Miller: at the same Time, I added, that, if he juged this Step necessary, I did not know whether, as Things were circumstanced, I cou'd be allowed to make Use of the only Argument, which had been before serviceable viz that I was the Object of M[iss] M[iller]'s Choice. In his Answer he advises me to visit the old Gentleman—and proceeds—"Nancy says, you may make Use of the same Argument you did before. She knows no Reason why you shou'd think otherwise." And a little after—"Poor Nancy was taken with a Fever yesterday Morning, which continued all Day and Part of the Night. She has not been Company for any Person, since you left this Place. ["]

    In Consequence of *This*—behold me before Breakfast at Mi[t]chels ([Tuesday, Sept.] 9) in my Way to F[lower] de H[undred]. I was in Discourse with Mrs. [Susanna] Bolling, in the Passage, when Miss

Miller descended from her Appartment—Heavens! how changed! She wore a Face of Desperation and was so much reduced, that she sunk almost fainting into my Arms. I was never in my Life assailed by such a Variety of Passions. Love, Pity for the Object of my Adoration, and Resentment against the Authors of our Unhappiness, alternately took Possession of my Soul: I was hardly able to sustain the charming Burden, that had committed itself to my Support. She besought her Uncle [Col. Alexander] Bolling to attend me down to her Father. "Conjure him, my dear Uncle," said she, "to remember the Difficulties, he had to encounter in his Addresses to my Mother: Let him remember *them*, and, 'tis to be believed, he will not torture me so." The good Colonel agreed to go with me: but we saw, at Prince-George Court, a Gentleman, who occasioned some Alteration in our Resolutions. Mr. Bolling Stark was just returned from F[lower] de H[undred] and confirmed what had been wrote me concerning the Opposition made by James Johnson. He said, it wou'd be much better, if I refrained going to that Gentleman's Habitation, and that, the next Day, himself wou'd return thither with Col. Bolling. This was agreed upon. Mr. Baird was that Morning desired by Miss Miller to acquaint Mr. Johnson, that she wou'd no more consider him but as an Enemy. She never thought of him, I believe, at that Time, without Indignation.

My two Friends departed ([Wednesday, Sept.] 10) for F[lower] d[e] H[undred]. I passed the Time, during their Absence, in endeavouring to convince M[iss] Miller, that our Happiness ought not to depend upon the Answer, they might bring from her Father: and I wrought on her so far as to be satisfied, I might direct her Resolutions. This barbarous old Harlowe [15] sent us Word, ([Thursday, Sept.] 11) that if his Daughter wou'd go with him chearfully, and I wou'd engage to live in England, he wou'd consent to the Match and do every Thing for us in his Power. He wou'd not oblige himself to abrige the Term, he had before appointed: but assured me, he never wou'd do any Thing to induce her to break her Engagements. I was so sensible (whether this Declaration was or was not intended to dissolve them) that it wou'd in Reality produce such an Event, that I assured Miss Miller, (if she agreed not to conceal herself in a Gentleman's House, who offered her his Protection,) I wou'd not, on my Side, repair to Great-Britain. She complained of this, in the most pathetic Terms, to her Uncle: and continued for more than two Hours in a Condition, none but an Eye-Witness can conceive. This immoderate Grief operated a Change in my Resolution and I agreed to every Thing she desired.

It must be remarked, that, within two Days after this, I was no more received with that Cordiality to which, I had been lately accustomed. The little Cupids no more sparked in her Eyes at my Appearance. To this sweet Behaviour succeeded a constrained Kind of Civility, of which no one cou'd comprehend the Reason.

> O Dolcezze amarissime d'Amore!
> Quanto è piu duro perdervi, che mai
> Non v'haver o provate o possedute!
> Come saria l'Amar' felice stato,
> Se'l già goduto Ben non si perdesse,
> O, quando egli si perde,
> Ogni Memoria ancora
> Del dileguato Ben si dileguasse.
>   Guarini.[16]

Mrs. [Susanna] Bolling and Miss Miller went ([Saturday, Sept.] 13) to an Entertainment at Mr. Peterson's. 'Twas after 12 o'Clock before they departed from Mitchels. Miss Miller, tho' dressed betimes, avoided my Company, so that, 'til *then*, I was quite alone. As this Treatment was very unusual and very mortifying, it made such an Impression on me as may be guessed. I attended the Ladies to Peterson's and went thence to Mr. Murray's. Mr. Black arrived there, soon after, and acquainted me, that he had seen the Messenger, dispatched by Mr. Miller to order his Children to F[lower] de H[undred]. They were to sail the Tuesday [Sept. 16] following—*that* being Saturday [Sept. 13]. This Information produced my immediate Return to Peterson's. Miss Miller astonished me, on hearing the Matter, by answering *"Im glad of it."* I desired to have some Conversation with her in the Evening, but that cou'd not be granted, she being indisposed: a Circumstance, which had not, a few Days before, prevented my Admission. I then opened my Heart to Mrs. Bolling and intreated her to obtain an Explanation of a Reserve, that filled me with

Uneasiness. Miss Miller answered, in the strongest Terms, that she was unchanged: and I was as dear to her as ever. She moreover said (which did not well quadrate with her former Declaration) that she had not been herself, since she heard of her Father's Message. I was obliged to digest some bitter Pills the next Day, the last we were to be together at Mitchels. However she was not quite insufferable, and gave me several little Marks of her Esteem. When the Family retired at Night, I attended her into her Chamber and continued some Time in Conversation. I upbraided her, in the most tender Manner, with her Indifference: and beg'd to know whether I had any Thing to apprehend from her Want of Perseverence. Her Reply was "I swear you are very affronting: how can you suspect me of so little Steadiness?" These were her proper Expressions. I took Leave after the warmest Embraces. [Monday] September 15. 1760 Col. Bolling, his Wife, Miss Miller, &c. and myself departed from Mitchels. Our Voyage was very disagreeable, as the Ladies were much frighted and Miss Miller more indifferent than ever. We arrived at F[lower] de H[undred] about 2 o Clock. *There* were many Gentlemen from Petersburgh and elsewhere so that I cou'd have no Conversation with Mr. Miller. I went in the Evening to Mr. Morrison's, where I passed the Night and returned the next Day, the to me famous

[Tuesday] 16 of September,
while the Company were at Breakfast. C[olonel Alexander] Bolling, being soonest done, walked with me and acquainted me with the Observations, he had made, as well as myself, on Miss Miller's Behaviour: in Consequence of which, I resolved to come to an Explanation; but, having an Opportunity to speak to her Father before I cou'd get one to speak to herself, I besought him to give me some Assurance, that he wou'd consent to our Union as soon as I cou'd arrive in England in the Spring. This he absolutely refused. On my leaving him I found Miss Miller, seated in a large Windsor Chair in the Piazza. I sat down by her, and, after informing her how Matters stood, desired to know whether she wou'd correspond with me closely, after her Arrival in great Britain. "She did not know." "The Coldness of your late Behaviour gives me the greatest Uneasiness: tell me, I beseech you, Madam, whether y[ou]r Sentiments or Resolutions are changed, with Respect to me?"

"My *Sentiments* are not changed."

A particular Stress, being laid on the word *Sentiments*, implied a Changement in her Resolutions.

"Madam, I am quite amazed: answer me this, my Nancy; must I consider myself as under an Engagement to you? Assure yourself, that no Promises from you will be esteemed binding by me, if you chuse they shou'd be otherwise."

"I can't answer that Question, 'til I speak with my Daddy."

"It depends then on your Father! Indeed, my Nancy, I did not think it possible."

I arose and walked in the Garden. She seemed much moved. After having made some Turns, I returned into the Piazza, where I found her in close Conversation with James Johnson, who, she well knew, wou'd do every Thing in his Power to dissolve our Engagements. And, in Effect, he succeeded but too well. He insinuated to her, that Mr. Miller had personal Objections to me and that, for the ensuing two Years, we were to have no Manner of Communication whatever: both which Assertions were contrary to that Gentleman's repeated Declarations. I continued my Walk and in a few Minutes returned a second Time. Miss Miller then started up and retired, with great Marks of Confusion, to her Chamber.

Mrs. [Susanna] Bolling acquainted me, at her [Anne Miller's] Desire, "that she wished our Contract might terminate; for that, being satisfied of her Father's Aversion to the Match, she never wou'd marry a Man, that was disagreeable to him."

Mrs. Bolling afterwards denied having ever delivered this Message.[17]

This Excuse will appear, to any one who has read the preceding Pages, altogether frivolous. This Girl, who, eight Days before, wou'd weep, nay appear in Agonies at the least Doubt, I might intimate of her Constancy, did not blush to desire me, by Mrs. Bolling, to return her the letter she wrote her Father, requesting his Consent to her Continuance in this Colony and telling him it was on that her whole Happiness depended.

"If Miss Miller will come in Person and ask for that Letter, be assured, Madam, it shall be sent her." This was a Task to which she was not equal.

"She cou'd not see me," she said and I believed it; 'twas bad enough to part in that Manner: much worse—to take a formal Leave.

This, Sir [i.e., "R.B." (Robert Beverley?)], is a Detail of every Thing that passed between Miss Miller and myself; for I departed from F[lower] de H[undred] immediately. What remains, and even this will fill much Paper, is nothing more than the Substance of several Informations, I received from different Persons; and which are no otherwise interesting, than as they may serve to conduct M[iss] M[iller] quite out of a Country, the Esteem of which she has so indiscreetly forfeited. I shall comfort myself with never having deserved such unworthy Treatment, and govern myself by Horace's good old Maxim, that

> Levius fit Patientiâ
> Quioquid corrigere est Nefas;[18]

And wait, with all the Patience of a Philosopher, for the Completion of Buchanan's Observation,

> Tristia secundis, et secunda tristibus
> Vicissitudo acerba Sortis temperat.[19]

In the mean Time I am, with great Sincerity, Sir, your,

very affectionate Servt

Bolling jun.

P. S.

After Colonel Bolling's Return to Mitchels ([Thursday, Sept.] 18) I waited on him not without Hopes, I own, of having some agreeable Message from my Butterfly. His Wife and himself informed me, that after my Departure, she was much affected, threw herself backward on the Bed and continued in that Situation great Part of the Afternoon: That they left her the next Day on Board the filthiest Vessel in the World in a State of Distraction, they cou'd not describe without weeping. When they took Leave of her, she clasped the Colonel by the Hand and with every visible Mark of Despair, "O my dear Uncle," said she, "what wou'd I give to return with you! O I wou'd give the whole World," and immediately ran off the Deck into her Cabbin, making Lamentations, that might be heard all over the Ship; her Father, who was present, being the only Person unaffected. She still declared, that I was and ever wou'd be the Object of her Inclination. A Lock of her Hair was delivered me, I suppose by way of Compromise for the whole which I ought to have received.

Mr. Baker saw her after this: but he avoided entering into any Conversation with her, as he was sensible, he cou'd not moderate, as he ought, his irascible Faculties. He described her with Indignation as resigned to the Direction of James Johnson and perfectly reconciled to her Destiny. In Consequence of this Information I wrote her a Letter (to be delivered her in Glasgow by Capt McLachlan) in which after describing the Uneasiness some of her Friends were under at hearing the Circumstances of her Embarkation—I proceed—

From such a Beginning (viz. the excessive Melancholy of the Company) I cou'd form to myself no very pleasant Prospect for the Afternoon: but, strange Revolution! these ghastly Countenances cleared up, immediately after a general Overflowing. There certainly never was, *but once,* a more sudden Metamorphosis. This was brought about by a Description of your Cabbin & &, which diverted every Body better than myself: who pretend not to eradicate, with such admirable Expedition, Sentiments, I once persuaded myself, I never shou'd have Occasion to change but with my Existence. Some Reflections of a melancholy Nature began to obtrude themselves on my Imagination, when my Friend Baker restore'd me in a great Measure to *mine,* by assuring me of *your* Tranquillity. Cultivate, my dear, amazing Cousin, that happy Thoughtlessness, which enables you to be satisfied under the most mortifying Circumstances,—with the Loss of Country, Friends, Reputation! As to the Loss of myself—I do not mention it; for, as nothing obliged you to such a Resolution as yours at the 16 Inst[ant], the Thing was voluntary; therefore no Misfortune. Yet, dear Cousin, methinks, you might have accomplished your Design and my Destruction in a Manner something less glorious:

Hadst thou. my Nancy, when my hopeless Heart,
Submissive to my Fortune and thy Will,
Had so much Spirit left as to be willing
To give thee back thy Vows, Ah hadst thou then
Pleaded the sad Necessity, thy Fate
Imposed upon thee, and, with gentle Friendship,
Since we must part at last—our Parting softened;
I shou'd indeed—I shou'd have been unhappy,
But not to this extreme.

Tancred. [20]

Twou'd give me Pleasure, tho I protest tis mere Matter of Curiosity, to know whether you still are blind and still give entire Credit to that Scoundrel and foul-mouthed Incendiary—James Johnson. Permit me, tho he may be at this Time your Oracle, to vent some Part of my Chagrin against a Wretch, whose insignificant Pride and despicable self-Importance afford no less Matter of Derision than Surprize to every Observer. And indeed, my Nancy, did I not think him all this and more, what must be my Sentiments of yourself? Cou'd I believe, that your last Resolution was taken before y[ou]r Arrival at F[lower] de H[undred], I shou'd not only not be displeased at the Congratulations of my Friends, but even —— however 'tis a Thing, which, (notwithstanding your undeserved Coldness before your Departure from Mitchels) I can never believe. Yet this Resolution, taken when it will, is a convincing Proof, that you are at this Time better able to excuse your Cousin Betsy's [Elizabeth Starke's] Indiscretion than heretofore. As for Mr. Miller, I acquit him from my Heart. Wou'd to Heaven every Body had treated me with as much Candor as that Gentleman.

May you be happy: but be, my dear Inconstant, be more cautious; for you can never be more exquisitely cruel, than in your Transactions with a Person, whom once you called, with Pleasure, your
Sept. 30. 1760.   Bolling.

Mr. Hood came to Petersburgh ([Tuesday] 30 7[Septem]ber) some time after the above Epistle had been put into the Hands of McLachlan.

He was far from thinking M[iss] M[iller] composed. On the contrary he averred, never to have seen such Depression as appeared in the Countenances of herself and Father. He told me that on mentioning once my abrupt Departure from F[lower] de H[undred] she burst into Tears and intreated him to change the Subject, wishing from her Heart that something might happen to prevent her leaving Virg[inia]. Altho' her leaving to Chance a Thing which she might and ought to have prevented herself was undoubtedly an Effect of no small Weakness yet so far was I wrought upon by this Circumstance and much Curiosity that I desired Mr. Hood to tell her (for he was going Home with Capt. McLachlan) that I shou'd not regard her Declaration of the 16 Sept[ember] as her final Answer since she had to my Knowledge been deceived by James Johnson. At the same Time I desired him (if she was affected at our Separation) not to suffer the Letter to be delivered; there being therein some Strokes which to a Person of the least Delicacy wou'd be extremely mortifying. The *Peggy* did not sail 'til the 17 October: Miss Miller never once went on Shore and, as Mr. Baird informed me, expressed little other Uneasiness than what arose from her Detention in the Country. He had sufficient Opportunity to make Observations; as he was with her from the Time she left Flower-de Hundred til her final Departure from
Virginia.

APPENDIX.

Mr. Callan informed me, the 9 May 1762, that Mr. Miller had died at London and that his Daughter was determined to return to Virginia. A Letter from Mr. Baker informed me that that Event had happened in the February preceding. I wrote a Letter to Miss Miller which was sent in June by the *Margaret* inviting her to Return and promising, if she did no chuse that, to accept of an Invitation from her & go to England. I do not know I ever repented more ardently of any Step than of having sent that pitiful Letter: for I was soon after assured that in her Letters for this Colony my Name was never once mentioned. Mr. Skipwith took Passage with Mr. Taggart, as he declared, to offer her his Addresses. Her great Indifference with Respect to me rendered me intirely indifferent as to his Success. He left this Colony tho' in another Vessel sometime in the

Beginning of November. My Letter by the *Margaret* was taken by the French so that I suppose it never reach'd Miss Miller tho very possibly other Letters to the same Purpose might be conveyed to her from Col. A[lexander] Bolling's Family in October. In Effect that *was* the Case. Letters from her to C[olonel] A[lexander] Bolling's Wife signified that a Visit from me wou'd be agreeable. In the mean Time, looking on her as married to Mr. The[odorick] Bland (which was positively asserted by John Bland just arrived from England) I turn'd my Vues and Affections to Miss Molly Burton of the Eastern Shore, to whom I was married, June the 5th. 1763, about 3 Weeks after the Arrival of M[iss] M[iller']s Letters in Virginia. This most amable Girl died in Child-Bed at Jordan's May 2. 1764. Miss Miller arrived in Virginia [   ] and was married to Sir Peyton Skipwith Bart: [   ].[21]

About a fort'night after she received my Congratulations at Prestwould both on her Marriage and Return to her Country that being the first Time I had the Pleasure of seeing her Face since the View I had of her Back at F[lower] de H[undred] Sep[tember] 16, 1760.

NOTES

Textual Note. Bolling's small volume, measuring 22 by 17 cm, contains six prefatory pages, 39 numbered pages containing the journal, one final unnumbered page of the journal, and two unnumbered pages of the Appendix. The volume is sewn, and probably once had a cover, but does not now, so that the ink in the prefatory poem from Tasso is partially worn way, and the page itself is quite dirty and consequently difficult to decipher. Except for "Canzonetta de Chiabrera" on pp. [ii–iii], the manuscript appears to be a fair copy, without the numerous revisions that characterize Bolling's writing. I have not shown the few cancellations that are in the manuscript but instead simply print the revisions.

The volume is in the Tucker-Coleman Papers, E. G. Swem Library, the College of William and Mary. Because St. George Tucker's wife was Lelia Skipwith Carter Tucker, the eldest child of Anne Miller Skipwith and Sir Peyton Skipwith, one may suspect that the courtship journal would have been interesting to the Tucker family for personal as well as literary reasons.

Substantive changes: I have made one emendation. The note written sideways in the middle of the page before Anne Miller's letter to her father on Aug. 26, 1760, seems to read "which for particular Reasons I shos'd [chos'd?] [followed by a canceled word of six? characters] shou'd."

Changes in accidentals: Bolling inconsistently used periods after the titles "Mr." "Col.," etc. I have normalized them. I have also dropped the periods when he used abbreviations that I have expanded. Thus "F.de H." becomes "F[lower] de H[undred]." Other bracketed insertions are also mine. In the few cases that he did not capitalize the first letter at the beginning of a sentence, I have capitalized it. I have also added the parentheses in the phrase "my Plantations in Albemarle (since Buckingham)." Using normal eighteenth-century style, he opened every line of quotation with a quotation mark and did not close the quotation; I have regularized quotation marks to present-day conventions. When he let a period stand as a pause (e.g., at the conclusion of the date in the title), I have changed the period to a comma.

1. Bolling's epigraph is from Consigliero's speech to Torrismondo, act 1, in Torquato Tasso (1544–1595), *Il re Torrismondo* (Milano: Casa Editrice Sonzogno, [1921]), 28. It may be literally translated: "There is no sorrow so bitter and so grave that it is not finally mitigated by time, which is the consoler of suffering souls, the medicine, and the means of forgetting all evils."

2. The published version of this poem in the *Universal Magazine* (see poem no. 3) indicates that he was imitating Gabriello Chiabrera's poem beginning "Del mio Sol son recciutelli" (Gabriello Chiabrera [1552–1637], *Can-*

zonetti rime varie dialoghi, ed. Luigi Negri [Torinese: Unione Tipografico, Deitrice, 1968], 202–4).

3. Molière's *L'école des femmes* 5.4.1571–76 (Jean Baptiste Poquelin [Molière] [1622–1673], *L'école des femmes* [1662], ed. S. Rossat-Mignod [Paris: Editions Sociales, 1964], 136). *The Plays of Molière*, tr. A. R. Waller (Edinburgh: John Grant, 1907), 3:113: "Everyone knows how imperfect they are: they consist but of extravagance and indiscretion; their minds are evil, and their souls unstable; nothing exists more frail and more brainless, nothing so faithless: yet, in spite of all that, these animals are the sole concern of everyone."

4. Virgil's *Aeneid* 4.569. Virgil, *Eclogues, Georgics, Aeneid I–IV*, tr. H. Rushton Fairclough (1916; rev. ed., Loeb Classical Library, Cambridge: Harvard University Press, 1978), 435: "A fickle and changeful thing is woman ever."

5. "Selon moi": in my opinion.

6. Although Bolling's "Circumstantial Account" makes it clear that inoculation was common among the Virginia gentry, popular prejudice against it still existed. See the references in "Dalgleish, Dr. John," in the Glossary.

7. Evidently Bolling, like many colonial Virginians, had malaria. See Darrett B. Rutman and Anita H. Rutman, "Of Agues and Fevers: Malaria in the Early Chesapeake," *William and Mary Quarterly*, 3d ser., 33 (1976): 31–60.

8. Professor Emeritus Leo M. Kaiser of the Classics Department, Loyola University, Chicago, informs me that Bolling made a careless error for *fugiendo vinces* (in fleeing, you conquer) and suggests that the maxim (which may be Bolling's own creation) echoes Ovid's sentiment in the *Ars Amatoria* 2.197, "Cedendo victor abibis." Ovid wrote "cede repugnanti: cedendo victor abibis": "Yield if she resists; by yielding you will depart the victor" (*The Art of Love and Other Poems*, tr. J. H. Zoyley, 2d ed., rev. G. P. Gould, Loeb Classical Library [Cambridge: Harvard University Press, 1979]: 78–79).

9. "Douceur": sweetness, meekness, or good nature.

10. Bolling published this poem under the title "The Flamers" in the *London Magazine* 33 (Feb. 1764): 101. An earlier version, entitled "On M[ary] A[nne] Randolph" appeared in the *Imperial Magazine* 3 (Oct. 1962): 538. See below, poem no. 1, for a discussion.

11. *"Comme un Coup de Foudre":* like a thunderbolt.

12. Torquato Tasso, *Aminta* (1580), 1.2.276–80, ed. Sarah D'Alberti (New York: S. T. Vanni, 1967), p. 32. Torquato Tasso, *Aminta Englisht: The Henry Reynolds Translation*, ed. Clifford Davidson (Fennimore, Wis.: John Weslburg, 1972), 12: "For mayds so inconstant ar of disposition, / that as th'ar soone at odds, th'ar soone wonne; / Uncertaine as the leafe blowne with each winde, / and flexible as is the bladed grasse."

13. "Consent, and not cohabitation (or coition) constitutes marriage" (*Black's Law Dictionary*, 5th ed. [St. Paul: West Publishing Co., 1979], 276). "Civilians" are experts in civil law.

14. Until 1752, the new year in Great Britain and the colonies began on March 25; under that system, September was the seventh, rather than the ninth, month.

15. An allusion to Clarissa's father in Samuel Richardson's novel *Clarissa Harlowe* (1747–48).

16. Mirtillo's speech in act 3, sc. 1 of Battista Guarini, *Il Pastor Fido*, tr. Richard Fanshaw, ed. J. H. Whitfield, Edinburgh Bilingual Library no. 1 (Austin: University of Texas Press, 1976), 176–77: "O bittersweets of Love! Far worse it is / To love, then never to have tasted blisse. / But O how sweet were Love, if it could not / Be lost, or being lost could be forgot!"

17. The handwriting and spacing show that this sentence was added later, perhaps at the time the "Appendix" was written.

18. Horace, *Odes* 1.24.19. *The Odes and Epodes*, tr. C. E. Bennett (1914; rpt. Loeb Classical Library, Cambridge: Harvard University Press, 1964), 69: "By endurance that grows lighter which Heaven forbids to change for good."

19. Lines spoken by Jepthes in George Buchanan's *Jephthanes, sive votum tragaedia* (*Georgii Buchanani Scoti poemata quae extant* [Amstelaedami: Apud Henricum Wetstenium, 1687], 205, ll. 39–40). *The Jephtha and Baptist*, tr. Alexander Gibb (Edinburgh: J. Moodie Miller, 1870), 61: "The stern vicissitude of fortune tempers / The sad with prosp'rous, prosp'rous with sad."

20. Bolling imitates Tancred's speech to his daughter after discovering her affair with Guiscardo, in the first tale on the fourth day of Boccaccio's *Decameron*. Bolling evidently knew Dryden's version, "Sigismonda and Guiscardo," ll. 339–46 (*The Works of John Dryden*, ed. Sir Walter Scott, rev. George Saintsbury, 11 [Edinburgh: William Paterson, 1885]: 438), as well as the original *Decameron*.

21. The two blanks are in the manuscript. Evidently Bolling had forgotten the exact dates of Anne Miller's arrival back in Virginia and of her marriage.

Bolling's Poems about the Courtship

Bolling's Poems about the Courtship

INTRODUCTION

The following seventeen poems concern either Robert Bolling's courtship of Anne Miller or the times and people that figure in the "Circumstantial Account." They constitute a supplement to and commentary upon the courtship journal; in turn, the journal supplies essential background for the poems. We know that Bolling had Anne Miller, James Johnson, and Hugh Miller in mind while writing most of the poems, for he used their names in a few manuscripts as well as in annotating his own copies of some of the ones that were published. Nevertheless, the poems do not re-create reality. The "Circumstantial Account" tries to be factual and incorporates exact places, times, snippets of conversation, and even copies of letters and other documents in order to prove its exactness and truthfulness. But Bolling's poems about the affair are semifictions. Their purpose was not to provide information for others, not to justify his own actions, not to record the courtship. Instead, the poems express his emotions.

In one case, he evidently wrote the poem about himself and Anne Miller but later added annotations that made the poem seem to refer to other contemporaries (see no. 6). In another, he wrote a version of the poem before his courtship of Anne Miller but revised it, applied it to her, and incorporated it into the manuscript of "A Circumstantial Account" (see "The Flamers," no. 1). And the poem he drafted as an epigraph to the courtship of Anne Miller was later revised and applied to his current sweetheart (who later became his wife), Mary Burton (see "A Canzonet of Chiabrera Imitated," poem no. 3). Even in those instances when he evidently had Anne Miller in mind while composing a poem, he usually was more interested in making the poem a good imitation of an

Italian poet's work than in recording historically accurate details of the courtship (see "The Departure" and "The Angry Lover," nos. 16 and 17). Indeed, one poem tells three entirely different versions of the love affair ("A Satire," poem no. 11).

Although the poems were not meant to be factual accounts of the courtship, Robert Bolling's Virginia contemporaries must have recognized the persons alluded to in published poems like "Hymn to Melancholy" (no. 5), "A Satire" (no. 11), "To Stella" (no. 12), and "The Dove" (no. 13). For his contemporaries, the published poems constituted the love affair's most public record. Of the seventeen poems complementing Bolling's courtship journal, six (nos. 1, 3, 5, 11, 12, and 13) appeared in print in Bolling's day—all in London magazines. And two of the six were reprinted in revised form in other London magazines (nos. 1 and 5). No manuscripts are extant for two of the printed poems (nos. 11 and 12). I suspect that some of these seventeen poems and probably additional ones appeared in the *Virginia Gazette*, but the *Gazette* is not extant for the early 1760s. Bolling dominated the extant Virginia papers during the rest of his life, and it would have been uncharacteristic of him not to celebrate Anne Miller in the Virginia newspaper when he was in love with her in 1760—and not to satirize James Johnson and Anne Miller in the *Virginia Gazette* when he was angry with them in late 1760 and 1761.

The great disadvantage of sending off poems for publication to London was that one could not be certain when they would actually appear in print. Bolling must have been chagrined when his old love poem to Anne Miller ("Hymn to Melancholy," no. 5) appeared in the *London Magazine* in February 1764. Because the magazine was actually printed in early March, it could hardly have reached Virginia before May. Bolling's wife Mary Burton (whom he had married on June 5, 1763) died on May 2, 1764, the approximate time of the magazine's arrival in Virginia. Around the same time Anne Miller and Peyton Skipwith returned to Virginia and married. They must have been as irritated at the untimely publication of Bolling's old love poems as the poet himself.

Fifteen of these poems survive among Bolling's manuscripts. Eleven are in his manuscript volume "Hilarodiana" (nos. 2, 4, 5, 6, 7, 9, 10, 13, 15, 16, and 17). Of these eleven, eight (nos. 3, 5, 6, 9, 13, 15, 16, and 17) are also found in revised form in his later manuscript volume "La Gazzetta." One poem, the "Letter to Jerman Baker" (no. 14), is unique to "La Gazzetta." Manuscripts of two of the poems (nos. 1 and 3) are in the "Circumstantial Account" itself, although "The Flamers" (no. 1) is a revised version of an earlier published poem, and the "Canzonet of Chiabrera Imitated" (no. 3) is a draft.

Several poems were probably not meant to be published. The poem on sleeping in Elizabeth Starke's bed ("The Dream," no. 2), the one returning razors to William Starke (no. 9), and the "Letter to Jerman Baker" (no. 13) were all probably too occasional for Bolling to consider revising them for publication. And the touch of the grotesque in the "Tragicomic Epistle to Roxana" (no. 4) and the personal vituperation in "A Prayer" (no. 9) suggest that Bolling did not intend to submit them to a public audience.

Bolling was a good poet. These early poems (he became twenty-two on August 28, 1760) are as competent as the general level of poetry in the English magazines of the day. To be sure, he was not a great poet. Few versifiers of any age achieve that rank. And none of these poems are as intrinsically interesting as his grotesque poem "Neanthe" (written c. 1762), his extraordinary occasional poem "A Copy of Verses in Praise of Winter" (Rind's *Virginia Gazette*, March 4, 1773), or his fine "Elegy" on the death of a number of friends at the battle of Point Pleasant (Dixon and Hunter's *Virginia Gazette*, May 20, 1775). Although these seventeen poems are not selected to represent his best poetry, several of them are technically interesting (note the unusual—and entirely successful—meter of the third version of poem no. 1 ["The Flamers"], and the unusual stanzaic pattern of poem no. 6 ["The Dupe"]). And they all shed light on the literary history of pre-Revolutionary Virginia.

The poems are printed in what I believe to be the chronological order of composition, but I have deliberately violated that sequence and included "A Canzonet of Chiabrera Imitated" as poem no. 3, even though it was probably composed after May 1761 (the date of "The Dove," poem no. 13); for I think the poems contained in "A Circumstantial Account" should precede the others. The dates of composition of eleven of the poems (nos. 2, 4, 5, 6, 7, 10, 13, 14, 15, 16, and 17) can be ascertained with some degree of certainty, but the six others (nos. 1, 3, 8, 9, 11, and 12) represent only my best guess.

Bolling flagged his own notes with a symbol preceding the annotated word; these have been changed to an asterisk following the word. Bolling usually wrote the epigraphs to his poems in an italic script; in those few cases where a distinction in script is unclear, I have used italics.

1

"THE FLAMERS"

Three versions of the poem survive. The first appeared in the *Imperial Magazine* 3 (Oct. 1762): 538 (Lemay, *Calendar,* no. 1886B), entitled "On M. A. Randolph." In his own copy of the *Imperial Magazine* (at the Huntington Library), Bolling added, just under the title, "by R. Bolling jun." The brief poem immediately preceding it in the *Imperial Magazine* is also by Bolling (Lemay, *Calendar,* no. 1886A) and is entitled "The Kiss. To M. A. R. O. C. I. R. V. I. A." In his copy of the *Imperial Magazine,* Bolling expanded the letters: "Mary Anne Randolph of Curles James River Virginia in America." Obviously "The Flamers" was also originally inspired by Mary Anne Randolph. Bolling probably wrote it in 1759 and sent it off to the *Imperial Magazine* early in 1760. This early version consists of conventional iambic tetrameter couplets.

The second version, untitled, is found in the "Circumstantial Account" (above, p. 61) just after Anne Miller's letter of August 26, 1760, to her father. The poem preserves the rhyming couplets but now has an unusual metrical pattern: the trimeter lines consist of seven syllables, an opening amphimacher and two iambs. The opening stressed syllable of each line gives the poem a vividness that suits its subject especially well.

The third version, entitled "The Flamers," appeared in the *London Magazine* 33 (Feb. 1764): 101 (Lemay, *Calendar,* no. 1961). It seems to me one of the intrinsically best poems printed herein.

Sources: I print two versions of the poem: the first version from Bolling's own copy of the *Imperial Magazine* for October 1762 at the Huntington Library and the greatly revised and superior third version from the *London Magazine* for February 1764.

[*First version*]
On M. A. RANDOLPH

Mal si compensa, ahi lasso, un breve sguardo,
A l'aspra passion, che dura tanto;
Un interrotto gaudio a un fermo pianto;
Un partir presto a un ritornarvi tardo.

ARIOSTO

See, from my lovely Stella's eyes
The forked light'ning, how it flies!
An arrow wounds in ev'ry glance,
And ev'ry smile a dagger plants;
Yet such united sweetness joins,   5
The wounded bosom scarce repines;
For that dear sweetness seems to cure
The woes, the flames inspir'd before:
It *seems*, alas! yet doth not heal;
Witness, my heart, —I feel them still.   10
PROMETHEUS

[*Third version*]

The FLAMERS.
SEE, from Stella's sloe-black eyes,
How the forked light'ning flies!
Arrows wound in every glance,
Every look a dagger plants!—
Yet such melting graces join,   5
Stung to death, we scarce repine;
For that softness seems to cure
All the harm, they did before.
Yet, in truth, it doth not heal;
Witness, Love, I suffer still!   10
PROMETHEUS

First version

Epigraph   From Ariosto, sonnet 2, ll. 1–4 (Ludovico Ariosto, *Opera minori*, ed. Cesare Segre [Milano: Riccardo Ricciardi, 1954], 129). The lines may be loosely translated: "The exchange isn't fair; alas! a brief glance of love / in exchange for a bitter passion that lasts so long / an intermittent pleasure for a long sorrow / a quick parting for a slow return."

Pseudonym   "Prometheus" was Bolling's most usual pseudonym in the early 1760s.

2
"THE DREAM"

Robert Bolling wrote "The Dream" at the Starkes' home, Broadway, Prince George County, in April 1760, while Anne Miller was recovering from inoculation for the smallpox at John Baird's in Blandford. A light poem in iambic tetrameter couplets, "The Dream" is typical of the occasional verse that Bolling frequently tossed off. One cannot be sure if the lovely subject of "The Dream" was Bolling's great passion at the time, Anne Miller, or if (as I suspect) he was unfaithful to her in his sleep and imagined himself with the usual inhabitant of Betsy Starke's bed.

Source: "Hilarodiana," 22.

The Dream

To Miss Elizabeth Stark of Broadway wrote
in her own Bed which the Bard took the
Freedom to occupy in her Absence abroad
April 1760.

When in your little Nest* I laid
When every Limb dissolved in Ease
Gave Entrance to what Whims you please
And Morpheus with my Fancy play'd
Me tho't within my ravish'd Arms   5
I clasped a Maid whose heavenly Charms
Surpass'd what ancient Poets feign:
Of Venus rising from the Main;
And lovely Helena's fine Form
Which raised such confounded Storm   10
As did proud Priam's Race destroy
And levelled with the Ground old Troy;
Or Cleopatra's red and white
Which gave great Julius such delight
That he, regaled by one so sweet,   15
Forgot his Forces and his Fleet
Forgot in Africk that his Foes

To fairer Expectations rose.
And equal Prospect at a Blow
To lay Pharsalie's Conqueror low.   20
     Her Hair of glossy Mouse was hid
With Ribbons might become a Bride
And wou'd to God she had been so
A real Bride not such in Show.
Her Eyes seem'd plunder'd from a Dove   25
Diffusing Sweetness Joy and Love.
Alas! a Glance of those fine Eyes
Made Passions strange within me rise.
Her Breath too—O Twas sweet as May
When bright Aurora gilds the Day;   30
The fragrant Woodbines in full Bloom
Emit a far less pure Perfume.
Her Bosom swelled—let Fancy tell
How did that lovely Bosom swell
But Fancy every Pow'r must stretch   35
E'er she its Charms sublime can reach.
     By all the Gods of fierce Desires
I could no longer stand such Fires!
But seized her to my glowing Breast—
And soon cou'd have described the Rest,   40
But cruel Morpheus slunk away
And show'd me how and where I lay.
                                        Robert Bolling

1   Nest*   *Bolling's note* Miss Stark was very short and her Bed almost as
short as herself.

7   ancient Poets   Hesiod, Homer, and Lucan.

8   Venus   Hesiod, *Theogony*, ll. 188–200, tells the story of "Venus rising
from the Main" (*The Homeric Hymns: Fragments of the Epic Cycle Homerica*, tr.
Hugh G. Evelyn-White, 2d ed., Loeb Classical Library [Cambridge: Harvard
University Press, 1936], 92–93).

9–12   Homer, *Iliad*, tells of Helen's beauty causing the Trojan War in
which Priam, king of Troy, and his children (including Hector) were killed.

13–20 Although the most famous literary version of Cleopatra's story is Shakespeare's *Antony and Cleopatra*, Bolling was evidently alluding to Lucan, *Pharsalia*, the story of Caesar's conquest of Pharsalia and his near death because of his dalliance with Cleopatra.

3

"A CANZONET OF CHIABRERA IMITATED"

Three versions of this imitation of Gabriello Chiabrera survive. Bolling originally composed it as a prefatory poem for his "Circumstantial Account" (above, pp. 47–48). He published a revision in the *Universal Magazine* 34 (Feb. 1764): 94 (Lemay, *Calendar*, no. 1964). Contrary to his normal practice (and the usual eighteenth-century custom), he signed the poem with his own name and dated it from Virginia. Evidently he sent the poem off to the *Universal Magazine* before he became seriously involved with Mary Burton in 1762, for he later revised the imitation again, substituting "Polly Burton" for the former opening ("Stella's waving"), and transcribed the poem in "La Gazzetta," 24–25.

Source: "La Gazzetta," 24–25.

A CANZONET of CHIABRERA imitated.

> *Del mio Sol son ricciutegli.*
> *I Capegli,*
> *Non biondetti ma brunetti &c.*

Polly Burton's Hair flows down
In a curl, not fair, but brown.
Blooming is her Cheek and shows
All that pleases in a Rose.
Polly's Lips beyond compare,   5
Foil the glowing Cinnabar;
And her eyes—by Heav'n her Eyes
Kill with Pleasure and Surprise.
Kill with Pleasure! —Poor the Phrase,
Mean Expression of their Praise!   10
Terms howe'er will fail, that's sure;

Spoke of them, all must be poor.
    Yet, since first I saw this Wonder
Peace and I have dwelt asunder.
La! When first I felt the Smart   15
Of that Urchin in my Heart,
Ev'ry where I heard 'em say
He did nothing but in Play.
That he wou'd not, no not he,
Wound the Finger of a Flea: 20
That from Venus he was born . . .
Horrid Falsehood I'll be sworn!
Never Goddess born was he:
But engendred by the Sea
On a Rock a Tempest tore   25
From its Roots and drove ashore.
Thence he learn'd (O baleful art!)
Greater Tumults to impart
To the human Soul than e'er
In that Element appear   30
When, broke from th'Æolian Caves,
Boreas sweeps the swelling Waves.
    True indeed—he sports and plays,
Has the prettiest little Ways,
Harmless, infantine his Air;   35
But—for Heaven's sake—beware.
Sporting—playing, I protest
We've no longer Heart in Breast.
    See him burst with Rage and Spite—
Let him Burst but I will write.   40
Little Viper, Dragon, Fiend,
Why, Peace-Breaker, shou'd I end?
Well thou knowest all the Pain,
Every Moment I sustain;
And, oerwhelm'd by thee with Woe,   45
Villain, must I praise thee too!

Epigraph   Chiabrera's canzonet beginning "Del mio sol son ricciutelli / i ca-
       pelli" may be found in Chiabrera, *Canzonette rime varie dialoghi*, ed.
       Negri, 202−4.

1   Polly Burton   See "Burton, Mary" in the Glossary.

16   urchin   Cupid.

31   Æolian caves   Where, in classical legend, the fierce winds, especially
       Boreas, are kept.

4
"TRAGICOMIC EPISTLE TO ROXANA"

Both the date of the poem (August 1760) and the speaker's pleading with
Roxana to marry him suggest that Orlando is a version of Robert Bolling
and Roxana a version of Anne Miller. Of course, the author's anti-
Petrarchan satire of himself as Orlando (which reflects his reading of
such Renaissance Italian poets as Francisco Berni [see Lemay, "Southern
Colonial Grotesque," 104−5]) might seem to clash with this personal application. But the "gumless Rows" of teeth (l. 10) and the "faded Cheeks"
of "tawney white and green" (ll. 12−13) are simply typical antisentimen-
tal and anti-Petrarchan touches. No expert in Italian literary traditions
would think that they were meant to be literally accurate. Yet they do re-
veal Bolling's ambivalent feelings as well as his self-satire. The poem was
not, I believe, intended for publication.
       Source: "Hilarodiana," 1.

Tragicomic Epistle to Roxana   August 1760

Orlando here expiring lies
Pierced with the Light'ning of your Eyes.
His Bosom heaves, his spirits fail——
I grieve to tell the mournful Tale.
His Eyes, those Rivals of the Snow,   5
In Streams, like Snows dissolving, flow:
His Nose, in Twist with foul Grimace,
Diagonally halves his Face.
His azure Lips beside his Nose

Uncase of teeth two gumless Rows,   10
And so the Bard with Pity speaks.
Above, below, his faded Cheeks,
In tawney white and green, disclose
Worse Ruin then e'er blasted Rose.
This goodly Frame (o Shame to tell)   15
Will shortly grace the Shades of Hell,
If you, ungrateful, still refuse
To join with him, the nuptial Noose.
Long since he'd been a Prey to Death
But that he still retains his Breath,   20
And, what we all surprising think,
Still eats his Bread & drinks his Drink.
Sure thou, Roxana, in whose Mind
The noblest Virtues Refuge find,
Whose greyhound Form and Lamia face   25
Conspire so well that Mind to grace,
This Son of Learning canst not see
Dying each Moment, and for thee;
Yet not relieve those mortal Woes
That give him more than Ætnas Throws.   30
O Trifler, as thou art, give Way
No more disdain Love's gentle Sway.

25   Lamia   In Greek mythology, a female phantom with a beautiful face but,
      from the waist down, a serpent's body.

5

"HYMN TO MELANCHOLY"

Two manuscript and two printed versions of this poem survive. The earliest appears in Robert Bolling's manuscript volume "Hilariodiana,"
10–11, where it is entitled "A Complaint" and where the poet noted that
it was "written a short Time before Miss Miller's Departure from Virginia, 1760." Because the *Peggy* did not actually sail until October 17 and
the last time Bolling saw Anne Miller was on September 16, the poem
probably dates from September 1760. The second version appeared in

the *Imperial Magazine* 2 (Oct. 1761): 552–53 (Lemay, *Calendar,* no. 1839B), where it contains an epigraph from Guarini. Bolling's own copy of the *Imperial Magazine* at the Huntington Library contains two corrections in the epigraph, two revisions in the poem, and the manuscript signature "R Bolling" at the end. Another manuscript copy, with further revisions, is extant in his manuscript volume "La Gazzetta," 28–29. And the fourth version, incorporating additional revisions, appeared in the *London Magazine* 33 (Feb. 1764): 101 (Lemay, *Calendar,* no. 1960).

In iambic tetrameter couplets, the poem addresses a personification of melancholy, the poet lamenting the departure of his love, cursing the "trembling culprit" responsible (James Johnson, one assumes), and ending with a prayer for the happiness of "Stella" (Anne Miller).

Source: London Magazine 33 (Feb. 1764): 101.

HYMN *to* MELANCHOLY.

Inscribed to Miss A. MILLER, of V.
Fuggi'l sereno e'l verde;
Non t'appressar ove sia riso o canto,
Canzon mia, no, ma Piante!
Non fa per te di star fra gente allegra,
Vedova sconsolata in veste negra.
PETRARCA.

O Melancholy, pensive maid,
Receive, within thy gloomy shade,
Th' unhappiest swain, e'er sought your aid!
To thee I'll mournful altars raise,
And, in sad dirges, sing thy praise.   5
To thy still groves and silent court
The wretched, of all times, resort:
And, when o'ercome by raging grief,
In thy calm precincts find relief.
With thee for ever I'll abide,   10
Nor, gentle goddess, quit thy side.
Since then no chearful ray remains
Of Hope, to sooth a lover's pains;

And 'tis decreed, and she must go; —
Then welcome, gloomy seat of woe!   15
Adieu the mirth inspiring smile,
And joys, that did my soul beguile:
Sweet pretty dreams of pleasure past,
Which I shall never, never taste!
Thou, Lord, who rul'st the spangled skies,   20
By whom the planets set and rise,
Great God, whom I with tears adore, —
O must I never see her more!
Alas! A few short minutes o'er
And Stella leaves her native shore!   25
Methinks I see the spreading sails,
Sad sight! impell'd by cruel gales,
Divide in waves the liquid plain,
And now scarce peeping o'er the main!
O Time, retard that baleful day,   30
Th' appointed term of Stella's stay!
The trembling culprit, (for his crime
To death condemn'd) thus dreads the time,
When, to avenge an injur'd land,
His country shall his life demand: 35
Thus, shuddering at each sound he hears,
Lives tortur'd by a thousand fears;
And, tho' he'll but the longer grieve,
Implores, like me, some small reprieve.
My Stella, since the fates decree,   40
That thou, dear maid, art dead to me;
This pray'r accept: "Ye pow'rs divine,
For Stella every joy combine!
From Envy's rage preserve her free,
And biting Slander's enmity!   45
O may she, in each climate, find,
A blessing, ne'er for me design'd,
With health of body, peace of mind!"
                              PROMETHEUS.

Epigraph   From Petrarch, sonnet 268, 2d ser., ll. 78–82. *Petrarch's Lyric Poems*, tr. Robert M. Durling (Cambridge: Harvard University Press, 1976), 440: "Flee the clear sky and greenery, do not approach where there is laughter and singing, my song, no, but where there is weeping; it is not fitting for you to be among cheerful people, disconsolate widow in black garments."

In the *Imperial Magazine* text, the epigraph is from Guarini, *Il Pastor Fido* 3.4.7–13 (omitting ll. 8–9). In Richard Fanshawe's translation of 1647 (which Bolling may have known), the passage is: "O ill starr'd Lovers! what avails it me / To have thy love? . . . / Whom Love hath joyn'd why dost thou separate, / Malitious Fate! And two divorc'd by Fate / Why joyn'st thou perverse Love?" (ed. Whitfield, 202–3).

6
"THE DUPE"

"The Dupe" survives in Bolling's manuscript volumes "Hilarodiana," 2–3 (where it is dated 1760), and "La Gazzetta," 33–35. At first the poem contained only five stanzas. The sixth stanza was added sideways in the margin in both manuscript volumes. Because the poems in "La Gazzetta" evidently were copied into that volume in the mid or late 1760s and "The Dupe" did not yet have the sixth stanza when it was copied, I suspect that the final stanza was added at least several years after the poem was originally written. The marginal identifications and concluding signature (none of which are present in "Hilarodiana") were evidently added to the "La Gazzetta" text when the sixth stanza was copied there.

In view of the late addition of the sixth stanza and the marginal glosses, I suspect that Bolling's identifications were deliberately misleading. Instead of being about Harry Beverley's courtship of "Miss [Lucy] Roy" and later of "her Sister" (actually her first cousin) Jane Wiley Roy (whom Beverley married), the poem is, I think, again about Bolling and Anne Miller. It is tempting to think that Bolling may (like Sir Peyton Skipwith after Anne Miller's death) have found himself attracted by Anne Miller's sister Jean, but Jean Miller was in Scotland during the period from 1764 to 1765 when Bolling was a widower.

"The Dupe" uses Bolling's usual metric line for light verse, iambic tetrameter; but the stanzaic form of seven lines, rhyming *a a b c c b b*, is quite uncommon. Ideally, it calls for two contrasting moods within each stanza, the first mood characterizing the couplets in lines one and two and four and five, the second mood characterizing the *b* rhyme in lines three, six, and seven. Bolling managed this difficult feat especially well in the last stanza, where the *b* rhyme is the slightly ludicrous feminine rhyme and where the last word in the poem wittily changes the tone and feeling of the whole.

Source: "La Gazzetta," 33–35.

The Dupe   1760

Non, perche a Mandricardo inferiore
Io te paressi, di te privo resto:
Ne so trovar Cagione a i Casi mici,
Se non quest'una, che Femina sei.
                              Ariosto.

I

Roxana once I lov'd tis true,
And she declared, she lov'd me too;
　　But o too soon my jealous Eyes
Cou'd see, that of her faithless Heart
Volpone had the greater Part,   5
　　And all her Vows to me were Lies:
　　O What cou'd equal my Surprize!

II

I said, Roxana, cou'd'st thou bear,
With me, thy livelong Life to share;
　　When that Volpone, happy Man!   10
Is all thy dazzled Souls Delight,
Thy Wish, by Day, Thy Wish by Night . . . ?
　　Indeed, Roxana, you'd sustain
　　But very ill the hated Chain.

III

The Fair replied, Indeed, my dear,   15
I blush such mortal Sounds to hear!
   And why, alas! you shou'd believe,
That this Volpone, whom you name,
Excites within my Breast a Flame
   That ought your gen'rous Love to grieve,   20
   I can't, indeed I can't, conceive.

IV

Convinc'd by Rhetoric so great,
I blest the Goodness of my Fate,
   Which promis'd me so fair a Maid:
And laugh'd within my Sleeve to think   25
How poor Volpone's Heart wou'd sink,
   When he beheld the Game I play'd,
   And saw his dearest Hopes betray'd.

V

The Term of Bliss long wish'd appears:
Behold me in my nuptial Gears,   30
   All Haste the beauteous Prey to seize.
But o the Devil take the blind!
The Traitress was already joind
   To curs'd Volpone. Girls, with Ease,
   Deceive what honest Heart they please.   35

VI

I was so vex'd . . . but let that rest,
Perhaps I may be quite as blest—
   Nay more than if I had not miss'd her—
Roxana was indeed most fair,
She pleas'd my Palate to a Hair;   40
   But now my Heart is all in Blister
   Consuming, burning for her Sister.*
Harry Beverley

Epigraph   From Ariosto, *Orlando Furioso*, canto 27, ll. 5–8. In the English translation by John Harrington (1591), which Bolling may have known, the lines are part of Rudomont's invective against women: "If reason could have led thy minde to prove, / Was Mandricard with me to be compared? / Reason hereof can be alledged by no man, / But this alone, my mistress is a woman" (ed. Robert McNulty [London: Oxford University Press, 1972]).

Stanza 1, sideways in the margin of "La Gazzetta," 33   *Bolling's note*
————Quantumque Amor sia se molesto
Che tutti i Marturelli del suo Regno
Dicano orn'ora: ahi lasso! io moro, io pero;
E'non si trova mai che cio sia vero.
Malmantile
Cant: 4, St. 1

This additional epigraph is canto 4, st. 1, ll. 5–8 of Lorenzo Lippi, *Il Malmantile*, 2 vols. (Firenze: Nestenus & Moucke, 1731), 1:303. Bolling's copy of *Il Malmantile*, with his armorial bookplate and annotations, is in the Huntington Library, acc. no. 129416. The lines may be loosely translated as: "However much love can be pernicious / So that all the little nincompoops of his reign / Say every hour, alas, I'm dying, I'm perishing— / One never finds out whether this is true."

34   After this line in the "Hilarodiana" text   *Bolling's note* Vide Henry VI
Evidently this is a reference to the character of Queen Margaret (Margaret of Anjou) in Shakespeare's *Henry VI*.

42   Sister *   *Bolling's note* Afterwards Mrs. Beverley

7
"THE LOVELORN"

The date of "The Lovelorn" (September 1760), its reference to "Polly's parting Breath" (l. 5), and its position in Bolling's manuscript volume "Hilarodiana" all suggest that the poem concerns Bolling's emotions following his last meeting with Anne Miller, September 16, 1760. The poetic meter is Bolling's usual iambic tetrameter. After the two quatrains of alternating rhyme *a b a b*, the concluding couplet is, as befits its meaning, especially stark. Bolling's music for the poem does not seem to be extant.
Source: "Hilarodiana," 3.

The Lovelorn   Sept. 1760
set to Music by RB Sept. 1766

1

Tis said indeed, but tis not true
That mighty Sorrows mortal are
And that if Life they don't subdue,
We well such gentle Grief may bear

2

I feel beyond Description Grief   5
It came with Polly's parting Breath
My Pains in Life deny Relief
Yet distant seems composing Death.

3

Alas! in so much Torture, I
Am scarce alive yet cannot die!   10

8
"THE USE AND DESIGN OF WOMEN"

This misogynist poem evidently dates from sometime after September 16, 1760. It is written in iambic tetrameter couplets and ends with a witty turn typical of the fashionable humor of the Restoration and the eighteenth century. The only copy survives in "La Gazzetta."

Source: "La Gazzetta," 1–2.

The Use & Design of Women
wrote on being discarded by my Mistress.

Credo che t'abbia la Natura e Dio
Produtto, o scellerato Sesso, al Mondo
Per una Soma, per un grave Fio
De l'Uom, che, senza te, saria giocondo:
Come a produtto anche il serpente rio,
E il Lupo e l'Orso: e fa l'Aer fecondo

E di Mosche, e di Vespe, e di Tafani,
E Loglio e Avena fa nascer tra i Grani
Ariosto net Furioso, Canto 27.

Th' Almighty formed Man and said
We have a noble Creature made:
Attach'd, perhaps too much, to Life—
Says Satan—Cure him with a Wife.
The great Creation's Lord behold   5
Now truckling to a haughty Scold;
Now see in Collin's downcast Eyes
The Slave who for Ritrosa dies;
The Soldier who disdains all fear
Accosts his Mistress with a Tear;   10
The Tar who brav'd a thousand Ills
The greatest from this Circe feels.
The warmest Friendships are disjoin'd
By this infernal female Kind
Who for our Bane expressly sent   15
Have far exceeded Heav'n's Intent.
Saint Paul the great Apostle says
That Matrimony merits Praise.
Yet honest Paul himself will own
It might be better let alone.   20
Then as the Plague avoid dear Boys
Connubial Ills connubial Joys
And e'er you take that Thing—a Wife
Consider of it—all your Life.

Epigraph   From Ariosto, *Orlando Furioso*, canto 27, st. 119 (in Ariosto's
    Opera, ed. Mario Apollonio [Milan: Rizzoli, 1944], 130). In the trans-
    lation by William Stewart Rose (ed. Stewart A. Baker and A. Bartlett
    Giamatti [Indianapolis: Bobbs-Merrill, 1968], 294): "I think that nature
    and an angry God / Produced thee to the world, thou wicked sex, / To be to
    man a plague, a chastening rod; / Happy, wert thou not present to perplex. /
    So serpent creeps along the grassy sod; / So bear and ravening wolf the for-
    est vex; / Wasp, fly, and gad-fly buzz in liquid air, / And the rich grain lies
    tangled with the tare."

11   Tar   The following line makes it clear that the sailor Bolling had in mind
was Ulysses.

12   Circe   The sorceress in Greek mythology who turned Ulysses' companions
into swine.

17–20   Bolling was alluding to 1 Corinthians 7:1–16.

9
"A PRAYER"

"A Prayer" attacks James Johnson, the confidant and adviser of Hugh
Miller. The poem records Johnson's supposed "Prayer" to Jove wherein
the Scot asks to be granted the power to interfere in others' lives. The
poem reveals that Bolling believed he and Anne Miller were of "equal
fortunes" (l. 37). The poem survives in Bolling's manuscript volumes
"Hilarodiana" and "La Gazzetta." Although undated, "A Prayer" could
not have been written before Bolling knew positively of Johnson's opposition, on September 10, 1760. I suspect that it was composed in late 1760
or early 1761. Bolling probably never meant to publish this poem of personal vituperation.
    Source: "La Gazzetta," 30–33.

A Prayer

O Spartan Dog,
More fell than Hunger, Anguish, or the Sea:
Look:
This is thy Work: the Object poisons Sight.
                                        Othello

As Johnson rose from Bed one Day
The Monster thus was heard to pray:
Give me great Jove a Neck so long
I may be known tho in full Throng
Six Feet or so great Jove will do   5
And I must have a Fools Cap too
With Ribbons well adorn'd that I
May glare and stare most mightily.

When e'er I speak a Word, great Jove,
Let all the Rabble round approve   10
Let every Cobler scrape and bob
For I wou'd govern e'en a Mob.
Whene'er a Man wou'd wed let me
Before yourself consulted be.
I am by vast Ambition spurred   15
To thrust this Nose in every Turd.
Such Influence let me have with all
Where e'er I ramble great and small
That none shall dare to go to P——
Or ventilate 'til I say yes.   20
On snarling Hugh I've fix'd my Reins
And am rewarded for my Pains.
Great Jove my Thanks; that blustering He
Is just the Fool, I'd have him be.
A Slave to Passion's lawless Rage   25
He woud the Devil himself engage,
Yet only rants when I command
And if I frown he'll kiss my Hand.
This well his lovely Daughter knows
Whose Bosom yet with Fear o'erflows   30
Her tender Heart confest the Fire
Of ardent Love and chaste Desire
And her Acasto felt the same
For mutual was the tender Flame
O Crime! O Crime! the horrid Plot,   35
Without my Ken, to pass was brought!
And equal fortunes, Age and Mind
Without my Aid well nigh were joind.
You know great Jove the Schemes I laid
You know the double Game I play'd   40
By these let weeping Conscience wonder
They're placed a thousand Leagues asunder.
    Thus let me live and widely reign
A Source of Terror Tears and Pain.

If Grief a hapless Sire invade   45
Or hardy Youth or blooming Maid
Then let Mankind apart all Doubt
In these or Terms, like these, break out . . .
This Tumble-Dough this Janus Face
This Foremost in the Devil's Grace.   50
This Wretch in Evil never paus'd
The new Disaster sure has caus'd
As Warmth from Fire as Cold from Ice
As Rains procede from cloudy Skies
From him procedes (detested Source   55
Of Ill) one settled steddy Course
More uniform than is the Day
Which drives the sable Night away,
More uniform than is the Night
Which next obscures the solar Light   60
If this you grant, all gracious Jove,
What more can your paternal Love.

Non è senza Cagion ch'io me ne doglio:
Intendami, chi pùo, che m'intend'io.

Epigraph   From Shakespeare's *Othello* 5.2.359–62, where Lodovico bids Iago to look upon the murdered Desdemona.

1   *Bolling's marginal note* James Johnson

21   *Bolling's marginal note* Hugh Millar

29   *Bolling's marginal note* Nancy Millar

33   *Bolling's marginal note* R Bolling
      The "R" is written over the "B" in the form of a monogram.

Concluding epigraph   Bolling combined half a line from Dante's *Inferno* 7.10 with a phrase of his own and line 17 from Petrarch's 105th *Rime sparse* (*The Divine Comedy of Dante Alighieri: Inferno*, tr. Allen Mandlebaum [Berkeley: University of California Press, 1980], 54–55; *Petrarch's Lyric Poems*, tr. Durling 208–9). The epigraph may be translated: "It is not without reason that I grieve over it; understand me who can, for I understand myself."

10
"TO MR. WILLIAM STARK OF BROADWAY"

This verse epistle of October 1760 survives only in Bolling's manuscript
volume "Hilarodiana." He evidently went to Williamsburg for the usual
social activities attending the opening of a session of the legislature (the
assembly convened on October 6, 1760), forgot his razor there, and while
visiting at Broadway on his way back to Chellow, borrowed an extra one
from his cousin William Starke. The poem, sent along with the razor,
apologizes for not returning the razor before. In rhyming couplets, the
poem is distinguished by its unusual dimeter line. The initial amphibrach
and a concluding iamb give the rhythm a jolting, lurching quality suited
to the supposed "puzzled, perplexed" mind frame of the distraught poet.
The several feminine rhymes add to the deliberately awkward and humorous qualities of the occasional poem.

Source: "Hilarodiana," 9.

> To Mr. William Stark of Broadway
> returning him Razors I had borrow'd and
> kept longer than the Term appointed,
> my own being left in Williamsburg.
>
> October, 1760

My Love-fit, dear Will,
Disorders me still;
My Mind is so vex'd,
So puzzled, perplex'd
That do what I can   5
I'm not the same Man
Since Nancy * departed.
I'm quite broken hearted,
And (o cruel Fate!)
Turn'd tender of Late.   10
My Memory's gone,
I'm lost and undone.
Miss Betsy will stare

And cry—Is that there?
What, shoh! Brother Billy,   15
He can't be so silly.
Run mad for a Thing,
That's now on the Wing?
Tis true, my dear Starky,*
But to the Point—Heark ye.   20
Your Razors, my Friend,
I tho't of—to send
But (thence is my Pain)
Forgot it again.
I'll down with my knees,   25
Dear Sir, if you please.
If then you look sour;
I'll down on all four.
For God's sake, Sir, pardon
A Wretch, Fate bears hard on,   30
Nor drive to Despair
A Wretch, almost there.
What tho' that huge Beard
At Blandford appear'd
Unshaved! Is that Matter   35
For making a Clatter?
Your Razors are sent ye'
My dear Sir, content ye.

7   Nancy*   *Bolling's note* Since Miss Millar to whom the author was engaged
    went with her father to Scotland. Scriblerus.

19 Starkey*   *Bolling's note* A familiar term given to Miss Betty Stark while she
    was yet an infant and continued by her Intimates after she became *Tem-
    pestiva Viro.*

       Bolling was alluding to Horace, *Odes* 1.23.12: "tempestiva sequi viro."
    Horace, *Odes and Epodes*, tr. Bennett, 67: "since now thou art ripe for a
    mate."

11
"A SATIRE"

No manuscripts of "A Satire" are extant, but the poem appeared over Bolling's usual pseudonym "Prometheus" in the *Imperial Magazine* for September 1761 (Lemay, *Calendar*, no. 1839A). Although the poet called the subject an "old affair which happened in the island of Providence," it is obvious to anyone who has read Bolling's "Circumstantial Account" that the poem is autobiographical. Within a framework containing an introductory apology (ll. 1–8) and a concluding misogynist moral (ll. 173–95), Bolling told four versions of his courtship of Anne Miller. The versions have an analogical relationship to one another (emphasized by the comparisons to the classical gods in ll. 154–64), each version testifying to the fickle nature of woman. Thus Sylvia, Roxana, Finessa, and Lucia are successive versions of Anne Miller; and Damon, Mirtillo, Philander, and Almanzor, versions of Bolling. The first tale (ll. 9–82) emphasizes the duplicity of James Johnson ("Old *Go-between*") who is ironically called "The honest man" in line 40. The second (ll. 83–98) stresses the exchange of vows by the two lovers, Mirtillo and Roxana, though she soon becomes enamored with Alphonso. The third (ll. 99–122) tells of the courtship of Finessa by Philander, his reasons for believing she loved him, and his disappointment. And the fourth (ll. 123–71) stresses the differences between the suitors "Brutus" (perhaps a version of Sir Peyton Skipwith) and "Almanzor" (a version of Bolling).

Source: Bolling's copy of the *Imperial Magazine* 2 (Sept. 1761): 495–96, at the Huntington Library.

A SATIRE
Respicere exemplar vitae morumque

> When times hangs heavy on my hands,
> And indolence the muse commands;
> What paper, then, good heav'n! is soil'd,
> And, oh! how common sense is foil'd;
> The raging pen, with speed immense,   5
> Leaves pages of impertinence,
> True pictures of an untaught mind,

To nothing, by just rules confin'd.
   Old *Go-between* my fancy strikes,
Whom ev'ry man alive dislikes: 10
A wretch, whose talent lies in ill,
Whose pois'nous lips a gall distill;
That truest merit will deride,
And firmest amity divide.
His heart no gen'rous passion knows,   15
No friendship in his bosom glows;
But, —Dev'l all—in him unite
The poorest pride, the bitt'rest spite,
The meanest envy, cunning low;
These keep the monster in a glow.   20
His eye-lids know no sweet repose;
But tortur'd with intestine woes,
He finds within himself the hell,
His crimes and arts deserve so well.
   That girl, who, with such luring smiles,   25
The *wretched creature's* soul beguiles.
That girl, 'tis now a week or more,
By the Almighty God-head swore; —
Nay, —hear her words: "O heav'nly pow'r,
Since such endearing ties combine   30
My Damon's glowing heart with mine:
As on this hope depends my bliss,
Bear witness, mighty Jove, I'm his.
The whales shall from their ocean rise,
With plumy wings, and lash the skies;   35
The birds shall sport beneath the waves,
And airy forms desert their graves,
The moon shall from the orb retire,
E'er other views my soul inspire."
   The honest man reply'd, Fair maid,   40
For he o'er heard what Sylvia said,
Pray say not so. I have in store

Such joys you scarce *conceiv'd* before.
I have, and you may take my word,
For you reserv'd a noble lord.   45
You, Sylvia, shall a title bear,
And in Britannia's honours share:
You, you, shall live where pleasures reign;
Far better *this* than *here* remain.

    "Why, *was* I sure, *good* Go-between,   50
To taste the sweets of such a scene,
I might, perhaps, infringe my vow:
But, is it possible?—pray how?"

    Tis surely so; but if, indeed,
This pleasing scheme should ill-succeed,   55
We'll take a *car-man* in his stead.
No *scoundrel* of thy *native** land
Can so much ready-cash command,
As *Harpagon*, whom often I
have tried, *in my necessity*.   60
For, five *per cent.* ten thousand pounds
He'll soon produce, —if you give bonds.
A man of temperance so great,
He seldom will sit down to eat.
Fear not that e'er a parasite   65
Will to your board himself invite:
With him the gnathos thrive but ill,
And may retire whene'er they will.

    "Your reasons, *pious* Go-between,
Are such, I'm sure, *as ne'er were seen*.   70
The Graces flow in all you say,
And steal my promises away:
Her ladyship would *sweet* appear,
But the *alternative* seems queer:
His *lordship's* or a *carman's* wife; —   75
'Tis wond'rous strange, upon my life!
Howe'er, his riches still *may* do;
But Damon, how I pity you!

So very rich! why then *be sure,*
Of Damon I shall think no more: 80
'Tis well, if he his senses hold.
Gods! how I love this carman's gold!"
   Roxana once great Jove address'd;
My love can *never* be effac'd,
Mirtillo is the *sweetest swain;* —   85
O grant he may relieve my pain!
Mirtillo felt the pleasing smart
Soon quiv'ring round his aking heart:
Behold him at Roxana's feet;
He did, and not in vain, intreat.   90
Such oaths they to each other swore,
Olympus never heard before.
Alphonso next the fair assail'd,
Alphonso's silver tongue prevail'd.
Mirtillo saw, —and left the dame   95
Enraptur'd with her *second* flame.
Alphonso heard, and quick withdrew,
What can Roxana want with *two?*
   Finessa seems to square her ways
By honour's laws, and merits praise;   100
The rules to which she'll *not* adhere,
Still graceful in her eyes appear.
Philander long address'd the maid,
And long she smil'd at all he said.
As *oft* Philander caught her eyes,   105
She look'd, as tho' 'twere by surprize,
And strove to smother rising sighs.
If e'er he told a tale, or sung,
She on the flowing accents hung;
'Till, from attention, she wou'd seem   110
Absorb'd in some enchanting dream.
Whene'er he danc'd, the wiley maid
With joy each bounding step survey'd;
And, when returning to his seat,

Her sparkling eyes persu'd him yet. 115
Secure of bliss, th' exulting swain
Presum'd to tell his am'rous pain,
But he, alas! *presum'd* in vain.
Finessa burn'd the self-same arts,
To practice on as heedless hearts; 120
And many pining bosoms bleed,
Who, like Philander, will succeed.
  Brutus, a youth of noble birth,
Was made, like chamber-pots, of earth;
Each word and action seem to say, 125
I Brutus, knight, am made of clay;
This clay is well wrought up with sand,
And forms a kind of thirsty land,
Which, when well moisten'd, will produce
The *devil to pay* among the *stews:* 130
But, as the soil requires manure,
He eats, O heav'ns! no mastiff more:
Whole dishes shrink beneath his knife,
He eats, as if he eat for life.
Thus have I, at some rustic shew, 135
Seen boys their hasty-puddings blow;
The prize, uprais'd, excite their zeal,
And each devour his scalding meal
With such rapidity, you'd swear,
Their future quiet center'd there. 140
With patience, Lucia, can you see
This monster of stupidity,
This senseless thing, by instinct led,
To claim the honour of your bed?
Can you, who so transcendent are, 145
Admit the hated booby there?
O Lucia! fraught with every charm,
A nobler breast than his to warm;
O! know thy worth, nor let a bribe
Engage thee in the wedded tribe. 150

With Brutus' bulk and opulence,
Compare Almanzor's form and sense.
Let Plutus once to Pallas yield;
Let fools to sages quit the field.
Venus to Vulcan gave her hand,   155
('Twas not by choice, but dire command)
And Hymen form'd the nuptial band.
But Hymen's bands were weak, for Mars
Had with this Venus sundry wars:
And once the heroes were engag'd,   160
The dreadful fray with fury rag'd;
When, shame to Mars, and Venus too,
Vulcan appear'd, the curtains drew—
But *hark!* what sounds invade my ears?
Why joyful every face appears?   165
Is Brutus then to Lucia join'd,
To Lucia! —*her,* whose gen'rous mind
Cou'd o'er ambition spread its wings,
And meanness hate, tho' found in kings;
When maids, like Lucia, judge so ill—   170
Let others act—*e'en how they will.*

   Be cautious, youths, nor trust your eyes;
Women at best are lovely *lies.*
What tho' perhaps some maid *has chanc'd*
To scape the censure here advanc'd?   175
'Twas lucky, that she trod a way,
From which she cou'd not go astray.
Thus adders guiltless on the beach
Repose, 'till something comes in reach.
The hawk, that yonder soars so high,   180
Is innocent; no prey is nigh.
No shepherd of the wolf complains,
That lies secur'd by bars and chains.
And flints are harmless, till the steel,
By contact fierce, those fires expel,   185
Those fires, which scarce less fatal are,

And, scarce less dreadful ills prepare,
Than that inconstant, faithless sex,
Ordain'd to rule, betray, perplex.
            Prometheus

Epigraph   Horace, *De Arte Poetica*, l. 317. Horace, *Satires, Epistles, and Ars Poetica*, tr. H. R. Fairclough (1926; rpt. Loeb Classical Library, Cambridge: Harvard University Press, 1966), 477: "Look to life and manners for a model."

57   *native* *   *Bolling's note* This alludes to an old affair which happened in the island of Providence. A young lady of that place was induced to break her engagements with a relation and countryman of her's, by a villainous go-between, and accompanied him to Great Britain.

155–63   Homer, *Odyssey* 8.266–365, and Ovid, *Metamorphoses* 4.171–89, tell of the marriage of Venus and Vulcan, her infidelity with Mars, and Vulcan's revenge.

12
"TO STELLA"

"To Stella" is known only from a printed version in the *Imperial Magazine* (Lemay, *Calendar*, no. 1881A). In Bolling's own copy of the magazine at the Huntington Library, the lover/persona Cynthio is identified as "Will Fleming" in Bolling's handwriting. I nevertheless suspect that the poem concerns Anne Miller and that Cynthio was Bolling himself. In the "Circumstantial Account" Bolling called Anne Miller "Stella" both in his prefatory poem (the imitation of Chiabrara) and in the brief verses following her letter of August 26. Besides, most of his poems from late 1760 (the approximate date of this poem) concern Anne Miller.

Source: Bolling's copy of the *Imperial Magazine* 3 (Sept. 1762): 481–82, at the Huntington Library.

To STELLA

So, Canzonetta mia, ch'avrai Vergogna
Gir cosi nuda suore,
Ma vanne pur, poiche ti manda Amore.
            Ariosto

Forgive, if while you pass each day
In social chat or harmless play,
While Cynthio breathes the burning sigh,
And you, with pain, his suit deny;
(From ev'ry bliss that sooths the mind,   5
Exil'd, and in a wood confin'd,
Where duller swains true joys forego,
And, for the pleasure, grasp the show)
I dare break in on thy repose,
And, how I love, to all I love, disclose: 10
How blest, if, while you read, a sigh
One moment join'd my misery;
And if, but ah, too much! a tear
Did on that heav'nly cheek appear,
And I the happy, happy cause;   15
What consolation to my woes!
But that dear face no grief should stain,
That heav'nly bosom feel no pain;
But sprightly smiles forever dwell,
Where sprightly smiles appear so well.   20
Yet do not scorn another's grief,
A tender pity gives relief; .
An order, which the pow'rs above
(Best present of their heav'nly love)
Have drawn on ev'ry gen'rous breast,   25
To sooth and succour the distrest.
Thy pity then, sweet maid, I claim;
Nor let that pity be a name:
Be more substantial the return;
O share the flames with which I burn.   30
Then will the pangs of slighted love
To scenes of endless joy improve:
This solitude, my charmer here,
A Paradise of bliss appear:
These groves, which oft in plaintive strain   35
Have sung my Stella lov'd in vain;

These groves, where melancholy reign'd,
Shall sing my Stella lov'd and gain'd.
Thus from appearances of woe,
Our warmest pleasures sometimes flow: 40
Dark clouds, which bode a tempest dire,
In harmless sunshine oft expire.
But, my dear Stella, if you give
To all my hopes a negative;
Appearances of endless woe   45
Oft in a real current flow:
Dark clouds which bode a tempest dire,
In dread Tornadoes oft expire.

Prometheus

Epigraph   Bolling attributes the epigraph to Ariosto, but I have searched for it
in vain. The words may be translated: "I know, my little song, that you will
be ashamed to go forth in this naked condition, but go anyway, because you
send forth love."

13
"THE DOVE"

Visiting Cobbs on May 21, 1761, Bolling heard the cooing of a turtle-
dove. This traditional literary reminder of a lost love inspired another
poem about Anne Miller, Hugh Miller, and James Johnson. The closing
(ll. 30–37) suggests that Bolling was recovering from his affair and suffered anguish now only when something recalled it. One notes that as an
American, he automatically called himself a "Rustic" (l. 32). In iambic
tetrameter, the poem is thoroughly traditional, but it has benefited from
several revisions. There are three extant texts of the poem: it is found
in his manuscript volumes "Hilarodiana," 6–7, and "La Gazzetta,"
29–30, and in the *Imperial Magazine* 3 (July 1762): 374 (Lemay, *Calendar*, no. 1873C).

Source: "La Gazzetta," 29–30.

The Dove

Notitiam, primosque Gradus Vicinia fecit:
Tempore crevit Amor: Taedae quoque Iure coissent;
Sed vetuere Patres.

                                    Ovid.

Sweet Dove, thy solitary Sounds
Restore my Soul its ancient Wounds.
Those tender Notes, as if of Woe,
Depress my lovelorn Bosom so:
Excite such Image, in my Mind,   5
Of Delia lovely, Delia kind,
That every Pang returns again,
And I repass an Age of Pain.
Thy Murmurs, plaintive Turtle, cease;
Such killing Scenes I must not trace—   10
Nor how, with Words, that speak the Heart:
With Looks, that ev'ry Thot impart: *
With trickling Streams of anxious Tears,
My darling Delia told her Fears:
Nor how her savage Father bore,   15
With Cruelty ne'er seen before,
And never to return again,
The melting virgin o'er the Main:
Nor how his vile, officious Friend,
(To gain that execrable End)   20
Coud to the meanest Arts descend:
O Crime! to break those tender Tyes,
Those Vows oft witness'd by the Skies!
Those killing Scenes, my swelling Breast,
Let those in long Oblivion rest.   25
But if perchance (so Fate decree)
Thou shoud'st this meddling Reptile see;
Then, o my Heart, just Rage display,
And his infernal Zeal repay.

Thus a clear Stream may gently glide, 30
While yet it's spacious Banks are wide:
No Sound the Rustic's Ear invade;
Unless soft Ripples lull the Glade.
But when, ere long, its closing Bound
Directs it's Course, thro broken Ground; 35
It's furious Motion pains the Eyes:
The Ear it's Roaring terrifies.

* *Pensosa mi rispose e così fiso*
Tenne'l suo dolce Squardo
Ch'al Cor mandò con le Parole il Viso.

Petrarca 94.

Epigraph   From Ovid's *Metamorphoses* 4.59–61. The translation by Frank
Justus Miller (Ovid, *Metamorphoses* [New York: Putnam, 1925], 1:183)
reads: "Their nearness made the first steps of their acquaintance. In time
love grew, and they would have been joined in marriage, too, but their parents forbade."

12 and note   Lines 88–90 in poem no. 119 of *Petrarch's Lyric Poems*, tr. Durling,
233; Bolling used "Tenne'l" for "Tenne il," "e" for "et," and "con" for
"co." Durling's translation (232) reads: "Thoughtful she answered me, and
so fixedly held her sweet regard on me, that to my heart she sent her face
along with her words."

27   this meddling Reptile   "his vile, officious Friend" (l. 19), James Johnson.

14
"LETTER TO JERMAN BAKER"

In the "Appendix" to his "Circumstantial Account," Bolling related that
he learned on May 9, 1762, of Hugh Miller's death. He added: "A
Letter from Mr. Baker informed me that that Event had happened in the
February preceding." The following doggerel verse epistle is Bolling's
reply to Jerman Baker's letter. The verse remarks on Hugh Miller's
death (ll. 44–49) and wishes "James Johnston [*sic*] was along with
Hugh" (l. 47). Baker also informed Bolling that Dr. Theodorick Bland
was courting Anne Miller. In this verse (evidently written in May

1762), Bolling hoped Theodorick Bland would not try to "steal my Girl away" but would instead woo "fair Dangerfield" (ll. 50–59).

The verse letter is filled with other news concerning the flirtations and courtships of the two young men. The first twelve lines comment on Baker's courtship of a girl of "New Kent," wishing him well. The next lines (13–27) say that "Fretilla" was still furious with Bolling because he joked about her hairy upper thighs. Bolling wanted to be friends with her again but preferred an open fight "To This Tranquillity of Hate" (ll. 28–43). After commenting on the news of Anne and Hugh Miller, the poem refers to Baker's joke about the "Jernian hat" (l. 60) and to his comment on Isabel Scot (l. 61) and suggests that Baker should tell these tales to "long Moll" (l. 63) or to a Spanish lady, "swarthy Vincent" (l. 65). Bolling closed the seventy-nine-line letter with a compliment.

Obviously Bolling did not labor over this verse epistle. It is doggerel, with only one phrase I admire ("Tranquillity of Hate"). But he copied it into "La Gazzetta" and ten years later, in 1772, made a few revisions, additions, and notes.

Source: "La Gazzetta," 89–91.

Letter in Answer
to one received From
Jerman Baker Esqr—May 1762

Your Letter I received, my Friend,
And much the Courtship recommend.
The Lord of Heaven loveth those,
He entertains with Cuffs and Blows:
Repentance comes where those aggrieve;   5
Then Pardon Men, of Course, receive.
    If you conjoin you with New-Kent;*
You'll pardon'd be; for you'll repent.
Go marry; tho no Grenadier,
You many a noble Poult may bear: 10
And Heaven will (if my Prayers can move)
Give double Portion of his Love.
    Fretilla still, with angry Face

Your humble Serviteur surveys,
And will, I fancy, all her Days.   15
Howe'er th' Offence I gave, at best,
Was but a dull attempt to Jest.
I only said, she bore, between
Her Thighs of Snow, a Parchment Skin,
Ill clean'd of Hair and crisp'd i th' Fire: 20
From little Cause what wondrous Ire!
But why so much she doth resent
Reflexions on her Tenement *
I can't conceive: you know, tis said,
That she no Man alive will wed: 25
Then what, I wonder, is to her
The little Matter's Character?
Dear Jerman, Id disburse a Crown
To bring that haughty Spirit down,
On Purpose, when twas low enough,   30
To give the Fire a second Puff.
Unless all Whalebone thrown aside
Her Smiles with no Reserve allied
Those lovely Looks she did restore
Where Friendship reigned as heretofore.   35
When banished from her Heart I saw
All Verjuice Id my own withdraw
Til then (I have my Nature, Sir,
As well as she) I wou'd prefer
To this Tranquillity of Hate   40
An active Caterwauling State
With here a Pinch and there a Scratch
And Things responsive those to Match.
    Old Hugh, it seems, if not belied,
Is gone to teach the Devils Pride.   45
For me, I wish (as much as you)
James Johnston was along with Hugh.
But then I believe they'd drive those Elves
From Hell and be worse Devils themselves.

The News, you tell, of Doctor Bland 50
I can't so clearly understand.
The knowing ones! pray who are they—
That say he'll steal my Girl* away?
God curse, I say, their Prophecies:
Be they the last of all their Lies. 55
Your Notions suit me to a Hair.
But how shou'd I such Jackdaws bear?
Shall Nancy's Heart before him yield
No let him take fair Dangerfield.
   Your Rubs about th'Jernian Hat, 60
Fair Isabella, and all that—
Pray take them back, and with the Tale
You sometimes may long Moll regale:
Or, if that Lady's in Disgrace,
And swarthy *Vincent* fills her Place; 65
With all my Heart—an Interval
Is long enough to tell it all.
Blest Scene, when, in her olive Arms,
In full Possession of the Charms,
(Which did, with such Applause; assuage 70
The glowing Lech of the last Age)
In Converse tender, social, gay,
The fleeting Minutes glide away,
Away, til Natures Pow'rs recruit,
And happy you can once more do't! 75
Pray bend my Compliments where due,
And think me, Baker, for 'tis true—
Of all the complimenting Croud,
Your Friend the warmest, tho least loud.

7   New Kent*   *Bolling's note* She was something passionate in her early Years
   but at this Time 1772 She is an admirable Woman, the Spouse of one of
   those human Beings whom God seems to have sent into the World to console
   those who read History, a smiling amiable but profound Philosopher.

23   Tenement*   *Bolling's note* She vindicated sometime afterwards the Reputa-

tion of the Affair in Question. She married and became the Mother of several Children.

47   *Bolling's marginal note* Millar

53   Girl*   *Bolling's note* Nancy Millar

61   *Bolling's marginal note* Isabel Scot

65   *Bolling's marginal note* a Spaniard

15
"THE EXILE"

Dated 1762 and addressed to "Sir Peyton Skipwith," the poem shows that Skipwith and Bolling continued as friends despite their rivalry over Anne Miller. The poem was written in 1762, evidently before Skipwith declared his intention of going to Scotland to woo Anne Miller. Bolling compared his country retreat at Chellow to Ovid's banishment to Tomas on the Black Sea. Thus Ovid's cultural isolation at Tomas (discussed in his *Tristia,* whence Bolling took the epigraph for this poem) was similar to the poet's situation at Chellow. Bolling invited Skipwith to visit him and drink his wine and hunt in the neighboring woods. The personal allusions in the conclusion are obscure. The two texts of the poem are from "Hilarodiana," 4–5, and, revised, in "La Gazzetta," 2–4.

    Source: "La Gazzetta," 2–4.

The Exile
To Sir Peyton Skipwith

1762

> *Si quis adhuc istic meminit Nasonis adempti*
> *Me sciat in media vivere Barbaria*
> *Sauromatae cingunt fera Gens Bessique Getaeque*
> *Quam non Ingenio Nomina digna meo.*

When banish'd Naso wrote he wrote
To drown the Pangs of anxious Tho't

Fatigued with Toil fatigued with Rest
He swore that Exile was no Test
He liv'd a wretched Life that's sure   5
For making of a Maid a W——
Hard Fate! For when a Lady's willing
To say I can't Ma'am is most killing.
Now when he plodded o'er and oer
His Volumes on the Getic Shore   10
Twou'd in some Measure sooth his Care
To think why he resided there.
My Case is harder far than his;
I never did a Princess kiss,
Have no dear Crime to please my Mind,   15
And never knew a Mistress kind:
Yet exil'd I to banish Tho't
Am forc'd to read what Ovid wrote.
An Exile too like his I have
At best, a better kind of Grave   20
Without Society, unless
With purling Rills and lisping Trees!
I see ('tis seldom tho' thank God)
To tell the Truth a two-leg'd Clod
Who tells me when I deign to hear   25
How the Tobacco fir'd last year
How Squirrels ate the Corn how Rust
His Hope of Harvest turn'd to Dust
So much for Company and when
He hath enough my Patience slain   30
To plaintive Ovid I repair
And read again with the same Air
I must believe old Shandy wore
When trigging at his monthly Oar
His Vigor met so rude a Shock   35
From Ma'am's Enquiry 'bout the Clock.
Dear Baronet thy prancing Steed

This Way, as usual, turn full Speed
The Wine Madera's Plains produce
We have: tho tax'd, 'tis pleasant Juice.   40
Here Woods where Game abounds invite
The Chace was always your Delight
Here other Pleasures you may find
And some of most voluptuous kind
Our Girls indeed are but so so   45
But Hunger is not nice you know.
The Marquis, late become a Duke,
May this Way take the other Look.
Miss Judy—let me whisper this—
Protests he now may take a Kiss.   50
In Charity to Chellowe fly
Of Spleen without your Aid I die.
What is my Torment Solitude
The—Ne quid nimis understood
With Change of Air may do you good.   55

Epigraph   Ovid's *Tristia* 3.10.1, 4–6, tr. Arthur Leslie Wheeler, Loeb Classical Library (Cambridge: Harvard University Press, 1939), 137: "If there
be still any there who remembers banished Naso . . . let him know that I
am living in the midst of the barbarian world. About me are the Sauromatae,
a cruel race, the Bessi, and the Getae, names how unworthy of my talent!"

Epigraph in the "Hilarodiana" text   Sine me Liber ibis in Urbim. Ovid.
      From Ovid's *Tristia* 1.1.1. The entire first line reads: "Parve—nec in-
video—sine me, liber, ibis in urbem"; "Little book, you will go without
me—and I grudge it not—to the city" (tr. Wheeler, 3).

33   old Shandy   An allusion to Lawrence Sterne's *Tristram Shandy* (1760–67).

37   Baronet   Sir Peyton Skipwith.

47   Marquis, late become a Duke   Unidentified.

49   Miss Judy   Unidentified.

54   Ne quid nimis   "Moderation in all things." Terence, *Andria* 61.

16
"THE DEPARTURE"

Between December 15 and 22, 1766, Bolling translated three poems from the contemporary Italian poet Pietro Metastasio (1699–1782). Two of the three, "The Departure" and "The Angry Lover" (to use Bolling's titles), evidently reminded him of his old passion for Anne Miller. I suspect that he translated them because they traced a course of love comparable to his own. "The Departure" translates Metastasio's "La Partenza." The early copy in "Hilarodiana," 40, is entitled "Canzonet to a Lady on Her Departure from the Country of the Author." Metastasio's poem evidently reminded Bolling of "the to me famous 16 of September," which, as he said in the "Circumstantial Account," was the last time he saw Anne Miller before her "Final Departure from *Virginia*." In his manuscript copy book "Hilarodiana," "The Departure" is the first of the three translations. (He placed it last in the revised copy in "La Gazzetta," 47–49, evidently to make it conform to the order in Metastasio.) He noted at the end of the three poems that he had preserved the original Italian stanzas in all three translations and kept the original rhyme scheme in two, although not in "The Departure," for "after all tis rather curious than desirable" to do so. Bolling's translation of "The Departure" by Metastasio compares well with that by Charles Burney, *Memoirs of the Life and Writings of the Abate Metastasio*, 2 vols. (London: G. G. and J. Robinson, 1796), 1:350–53.

Source: "La Gazzetta," 47–49.

The Departure
A Canzonet from Metastasio

Ecco quel fiero Istante &c

I
Behold the dreaded Instant
Farewell my lovely Nice
O what sad Hours shall I see
Thus severed from your Eyes
Sad Hours remote from Pleasure   5
With Woes replete o'er Measure

And you—who knows—alas!
May ne'er repass my Sighs.

II

At least allow my Fancy,
My fair one ever gracious, 10
It's lost Repose sequacious,
To trace whereer it flies.
Wherever Fortune guide you,
My Fancy waits beside you;
   And you—who knows—alas— 15
   May ne'er repass my Sighs.

III

In these far Climes I'll wander
With gloomy Steps o'er Mountains
And ask the Groves and Fountains
Where hers my Nice plies 20
The Ev'n shall hear and Morning
Your Name and Ev'n returning.
   And you—who knows—alas—
   May ne'er repass my sighs.

IV

How oft shall I revisit 25
Those Regions most endearing,
Sweet Scenes of Joy past bearing,
When Nice blest mine Eyes.
Each tender Recollection
Will fill me with Dejection. 30
   And you—who knows—alas—
   May ne'er repass my Sighs.

V

There's (I shall say) the Bower
Where glowed my Fair's Resentment

Which, *after*, (O Contentment!)   35
Gave Place to milder Skies.
Here Hope appear'd my Anguish;
There sweetly we did languish.
   And you—who knows—alas—
   May ne'er repass my Sighs.   40

VI

What Youths (on your Arrival,
Dear Maid, at your new Dwelling)
What Youths will—aye—be telling
The Feelings Love supplies.
O Gods! who knows, while warmer   45
They press my list'ning Charmer.
   Who knows, who knows—alas
   You'll e'er repass my Sighs.

VII

Reflect, in my poor Bosom,
What tender Shafts implanted.   50
Reflect, howe'er enchanted;
Twas hopeless of the Prize.
Consider, from this Parting
My very Soul is smarting.
   And that—who knows—alas—   55
   You'll e'er repass my Sighs.

Epigraph   The first line of Metastasio's poem "La Partenza," or "The Parting"
(*Tutte le opere di Pietro Metastasio*, ed. Bruno Brunelli, 5 vols. [Verona:
Montadori, 1947], 2:780–82).

17
"THE ANGRY LOVER"

The second of the three poems from Metastasio that Bolling translated between December 15 and 22, 1766, was originally entitled "The
Brouillerie: A Canzonet / To Nice on Her Inconstancy" in "Hilarodiana,"

40. When he revised the text and copied it into "La Gazzetta," 38–42, he entitled it "The Angry Lover" and placed it as the first of the three poems. "The Angry Lover" traces the course of a lover's emotion from the time of his passion to a relative indifference to his former love some years later. Evidently Bolling found that the poem was true both to his own experience as a lover and to the quite different emotions he experienced several years later when seeing or talking about Anne Miller, now Lady Skipwith.

Source: "La Gazzetta," 38–42.

| The Brouillerie a Canzonet from Metastasio | The Angry Lover A Canzonet from Metastasio |

Grazie agli Inganni tuoi &c.

I

Thanks to your artful Dealing,
At Length I Breath recover.
The Gods on a wrong'd Lover
A piteous Glance have deignd.
I feel (o happy Feeling!)   5
Your Eyes of Shafts unquivered,
My Soul from Bonds delivered . . .
Hark Freedom and—unfeign'd!

II

Tis spent so far—my Passion—
My Heart so calm a Place is,   10
Love there in vain seeks Traces
Of Wrath in which to hide.
No more my Cheek Confession
Makes, at your Name, by Blushes:
Nor, when I gaze, e'er rushes   15
Along my Veins the Tide.

III

I dream; but you're not ever,
As erst, my Fancy's Object.
I wake; you're not the Subject,
That first imploys my Brain.   20
When Distance doth dissever
Our Steps, I scarce perceive it:
Returned agin, believe it,
I taste nor Joy nor Pain.

IV

I mention your Profusion   25
Of Charms, without a Pressure,
And o'er & o'er I trace your
Deceits; yet can't resent.
I feel no more Confusion
At unexpected Meeting   30
And e'en, my Rival greeting,
On you, with him, descant.

V

With haughty Frown survey me,
Or with benignant Feature;
Your Scorn, fallacious Creature,   35
Your Kindness I despise.
Those Lips no more can sway me,
Tho whilome so decisive:
Nor feels my Heart the missive
Effulgence of your Eyes.   40

VI

Whate'er offends or Pleases,
If grave I am or sprightly;
You mix therein so slightly,
I ne'er to you refer.
Without your futile Graces   45

I love the Groves and Vallies:
If not; your Charms & Sallies
Cou'd Scarce their Silence chear.

VII

Now juge if I deceive you
I own (for Truth's a Duty)   50
Still own you've wondrous Beauty
Yet not beyond Compare.
For (let not Truth aggrieve you,)
In that sweet Face I've noted
Defects, that, while I doted,   55
I held supremely fair.

VIII

When first, your Yoke forsaking,
I dared to live unshackled;
My very Heart strings crackled:
My Shame I blushing own.   60
Hard was that Undertaking:
Yet Torture gives Assurance:
To win one's self from Durance,
All Hazards may be run.

IX

To birdlimed Twigs adhering,   65
The Gold-Finch struggles mainly
And quits her Plumes serenely;
But gains dear Liberty.
Behold, new Plumes appearing,
She beauteous grows and wiser: 70
No farther Wiles entice her
To the forbidden Tree.

X

I know, you think still glowing
In me my former Passion,
Because, in long Oration,   75
I preach it's Obsequies.
To Instinct this is owing.
The Sailor tells, with Pleasure,
In Port & now, at Leisure,
His Dangers on the Seas.   80

XI

Returning from the Battle,
His Rage the Soldier mentions,
And, gained in fierce Contentions,
Displays each honored Scar.
The Slave enlarged will rattle   85
The Chains, that lately bound him,
And tell to all around him
The Woes, he felt afar.

XII

Their Motive is my Motive;
Self Pleasure: not a Moment   90
Heed I your future Comment:
Alike your Praise and Blame.
No Sigh breathes from me votive
Of your returning Favor,
Nor care I if you're graver   95
At Mention of my Name.

XIII

I leave an airy Rover,
You lose a warm Adorer;
I know not which securer
Of Comfort thus remains.   100

I know so true a Lover
No Fortune can make Nice's
To find—full of Devices—
A Jill, requires no Pains.

Epigraph   The first line of Metastasio's "La Liberta. A Nice" (ed. Brunelli,
    2:774–77).

The word(s) before the closing bracket are found in the copy-texts printed above; the word(s) after the closing bracket are the (generally earlier) alternatives. Only substantive differences (i.e., those involving words) between texts are shown; but editorial emendations of accidentals (changes of punctuation) in the copy-text are also listed, except for the changes of Bolling's various symbols for notes to asterisks.

1. "The Flamers"
For the three texts, see the introduction to the poem.

First version
Signature   *added in Bolling's holograph in the Huntington Library copy of the Impe-*
        rial Magazine   by R. Bolling jun
Third version. There are two differences between the copy-text and the manuscript
        copy in the "Circumstantial Account."
Title]   *No title*
1   Stella's sloe-black]   my lovely Stella's

2. "The Dream"
The only extant copy of "The Dream" is in Bolling's manuscript volume "Hilaro-diana." The manuscript contains no revisions. A blot, however, over the third word in line 11 renders that word nearly indecipherable. The word begins with a "p" and contains four or five more letters: the second, third, and fourth letters contain no ascenders or descenders. If the word contains only four letters, it may well be "poor." There is enough space for five letters, but the blot is strong over the fifth letter, which could have an ascender but not a descender. My best guess is that the word is "proud." I have added the punctuation in lines 7, 8, 12, 15, 26–28, 30, 32, and 38–40.

3. "A Canzonet of Chiabrera Imitated"
Three texts of this poem survive. The draft is contained in the prefatory pages [ii–iii] of "A Circumstantial Account" (a fair copy of the draft is printed above, pp. 47–48). A slightly revised copy appeared in the *Universal Magazine*. The third text, revised again, appears in "La Gazzetta." I have chosen the last as my copy-text, but to it I have added the following punctuation from the *Universal Magazine* text: commas after *curl* and *fair* (l. 2), *compare* (5), *Phrase* (9), *fail* (11), *them* (12), *Heart* (16), *When* and *Caves* (31), *plays* (33), *Ways* (34), *Harmless* (35), and *Viper, Dragon,* and *Fiend* (41); parentheses in line 27; semicolons at the end of lines 6 and 35; a colon at the end of line 20; periods at the end

of lines 2, 8, and 36; an exclamation mark at the end of line 10; and a question mark at the end of line 42.

The following notes show the substantive differences between the "La Gazzetta" copy-text; the *Universal Magazine* text (*UM*); and the fair-copy transcription of the "Circumstantial Account" (*CA*) text, in that order. The wavy dash or tilde (-) indicates that the same substantive text appears as in the preceding source.

Title]   -; Canzonetta di Chiabrera
Epigraph]   *third line lacking* ;   *entirely lacking*
      "ricciutegli" and "Capegli" are "ricciutelli" and "capelli" in Negri
1   Polly Burton's]   STELLA's waving ;   -
3   shows]   - ;   shews
4   that pleases in]   - ;   the Beauties of
5   Polly's]   Stella's ;   And her
6   Foil . . . Cinnabar;]   Deeper than Vermillion are; — ;   -
7-12   *Lines lacking in CA.*
11   that's]   I'm   *UM*
13   this Wonder]   all this, ;   -
14   Peace . . . asunder.]   I've not had a moment's peace. ;   -
15   La!]   Lord! ;   ..
20   Wound the Finger of]   Could he help it, hurt ;   Hurt the Finger of—
21   That . . . was]   And was of a Goddess ;   That from Venus he was
22   Horrid Falsehood]   That he was not ;   Horrid Falsehood
27   Thence]   - ;   There
27   (O . . . art!)]   - ;   among the Waves
28-32   *Lines lacking in CA.*
36   Heaven's sake]   - ;   God's Sake! Lads,
40   Burst]   - ;   rave
45   oerwhelm'd by thee]   by thee oerwhelm'd ;   -
46   Villain, must I]   Woulds't thou have me
Concluding signature in UM   Virginia.   Robert Bolling, jun.

4. "Tragicomic Epistle to Roxana"

The only known text is in "Hilarodiana." Canceled words follow the closing bracket. I have added the period concluding line 11.

7   in . . . Grimace]   drove from its resting Place
8   Diagonally]   contorted
8   his]   his comic
10-11   *Between these two lines Bolling first wrote a couplet, a revised version of*

which he wrote below, as ll. 13–14   In Tawney white and Green disclose / Worse Ruin than e'er fell a Rose

5. "Hymn to Melancholy"

There are four known texts. The earliest, in Bolling's manuscript volume "Hilarodiana," is much revised and evidently dates from about September 1760. Its title is given as "A Complaint written a short Time before Miss Millar's Departure from Virginia," and its epigraph consists of the five lines from Petrarch used in the final version, the copy-text. A revised, fair copy of this version appeared in the *Imperial Magazine*. Bolling revised the poem again when he copied it into "La Gazzetta." He made further manuscript revisions in the "La Gazzetta" copy, probably about 1763, and sent off a fair copy to the *London Magazine*, where it appeared as the lead poem (and the first of three poems by him) in that issue of the magazine. He had changed the title, added the subtitle "Inscribed to Miss A. Miller, of V.," dropped the last sentimental twelve lines, and signed it "Prometheus."

The textual notes show all the substantive changes between the *London Magazine* text (the copy-text) and the version printed in Bolling's own copy of the *Imperial Magazine* at the Huntington Library.

Title HYMN . . .] *The* COMPLAINT.
Epigraph in Imperial Magazine
>   *O Anime in Amor, troppo infelici!*
>   *Perche, crudo* [corrected by hand from *crude*] *Destino,*
>   *Ne desunsci* [corrected by hand from *desuezisci*] *s'Amor ne, stringe?*
>   *E tu, perche ne stringi,*
>   *Se ne parte il Destin, perfido Amore!*
>   *Il Past. fido di Guarini.*

3   e'er sought your aid!]   that love e'er made.   [*Revised by hand to*] e'er . . . aid
5   And, in sad]   In solemn
8   when]   those,
8   by]   with
12 then . . . remains]   now, alas! no hopes appear
13 Of . . . pains;]   A deeply-tortur'd mind to chear;
14 And]   For,
14 and she]   The fair
19 shall never]   again, shall
20 Lord]   power
22 God]   Jove
23 O]   What—   [*Revised by hand to*] O

23–24 *Between these two lines, Imperial Magazine has the following couplet*
      O rather take that life you gave, / And cast my body to the grave!
25 Stella] Sylvia
28 Divide in waves] Glide swiftly o'er
29 And now scarce peeping o'er] Now scarce distinguish'd from
30–31 *No comparable lines in Imperial Magazine text*
33 dreads] sees
39 small] short
40 Stella] Sylvia
41 maid, art dead to] nymph, must part from
43 Stella] Sylvia
49–60 *lacking*]
    And O, could I this wish obtain,
    When distant climes my fair detain,   50
    That sometimes, from the world retir'd,
    Her soul with gentle warmth inspir'd,
    She'd think, and drop one tender tear,
    Her lovely self and fate severe;
    And wish, nor let the wish be vain,   55
    We still might live to meet again:
    'Twould, dearest Sylvia, sooth the woes,
    With which my wounded bosom glows;
    'Twould every painful thought countroul,
    And pour sweet comfort on my soul   60

6. "The Dupe"

The poem is known only from Bolling's manuscript volumes "Hilarodiana" and "La Gazzetta." Because the copy-text ("La Gazzetta") has little punctuation, I have added the punctuation from "Hilarodiana" and have capitalized the first words of lines 15 and 35 ("Indeed" and "Deceive"). Substantive differences in "Hilarodiana" are given after the closing bracket. The angle brackets indicate cancellations.

1 Roxana] Miss Roy
5 Volpone] Almanzor
10 Volpone] Almanzor
18 Volpone] Almanzor
29 The Term of Bliss] The ⟨Days⟩ Term of Joy
30 in my] ⟨in my⟩ wrapped in
34 curs'd Volpone] damn'd Almanzor
34 *written after this line in "Hilarodiana"* Vide Henry VI

35   *This line originally completed the poem in both "Hilarodiana" and "La Gaz-*
     zetta," but then Bolling added the last stanza sideways in both copybooks.
40   Palate]   Fancy

7. "The Lovelorn"

The only known text is in "Hilarodiana." There are no revisions in the manuscript.

8. "The Use and Design of Women"

The only known copy is in "La Gazzetta." It has just one revision. There are,
however, three differences between Bolling's epigraph from Ariosto and the version in Ariosto's *Opera*, ed. Appolonio, 130. I have added terminal punctuation
to lines 6, 8, 10, 16, and 18.

Epigraph
  2   scellerato]   scelerato
  5   a]   ha
  5   anche]   anco
23   take . . . a]   grapple with this

9. "A Prayer"

The poem survives in "Hilarodiana," and in a revised form in "La Gazzetta"
(my copy-text); the textual notes record all the substantive differences. Because
Bolling hardly punctuated the text in "La Gazzetta," I have added the periods
concluding lines 8, 12, and 22 from the text in "Hilarodiana"; and I have added
the parentheses in lines 55–56.

 6   have]   beg
19   p——]   piss
21   fix'd]   placed
23   blustering]   mighty
34   the]   their
35   O Crime! O Crime! the horrid Plot]   This! This! o horrid Crime was
     done
36   Without my Ken, to pass was brought!]   O Deathless Rage to me not
     known
37–38   *No comparable lines in "Hilarodiana"*
48   Terms, like these]   Such like Words
49   Dough]   dung
50   Foremost in the Devil's]   Object of Belphegor's
61   all gracious]   impartial

10. "To Mr. William Stark of Broadway"

The only known text is in "Hilarodiana." I have added punctuation in lines 2, 3, 4, 7, 8, 10, 11, 12, 19, 21, 23, and 30. Bolling drafted two incomplete different and longer versions of lines 15–18 in the margins. Because they are drafts and because I am uncertain of some readings in them, I do not print them. There are no other revisions in the manuscript.

11. "A Satire"

The only known text appears in the *Imperial Magazine*. As copy-text, I use Bolling's own copy of the *Imperial Magazine* at the Huntington Library, where he made the following four revisions or corrections (the words before the closing bracket are his corrections).

11   wretch]   wench
14   amity]   unity
137   excite]   excites
138   devour]   devours

In addition, Bolling scratched out his pseudonym *"Prometheus"* after the conclusion, but I retain it. I have added the closing quotation mark at the end of line 83.

12. "To Stella"

The only known text of "To Stella" is in the *Imperial Magazine*. Bolling's own copy of the *Imperial Magazine* at the Huntington Library bears three revisions and a note by Bolling, and I have made one substantive emendation.

3   Cynthio]   Will Fleming [*Bolling's note*]
11   a]   or [*Bolling's revision*]
13   too]   to
47   a]   the [*Bolling's revision*]
48   dread Tornadoes]   dreadful whirlwinds [*Bolling's revision*]

13. "The Dove"

"The Dove" exists in three versions. All have the same epigraph, but the titles differ. The earliest, dated "Cobbs, May 24, 1761," is in Bolling's manuscript volume "Hilarodiana," where its title is given as "Palinodia on hearing the cooing of a Dove." A revised version with the title "To a Turtle-Dove" appeared in the *Imperial Magazine* 3 (July 1762): 374 (Lemay, *Calendar*, no. 1873C), signed "Prometheus." It is one of five poems by Bolling in this issue of the *Imperial Magazine*. The third and last version is in his manuscript volume "La

Gazzetta." The last has a number of manuscript revisions and adds a note calling attention to a Petrarchan echo.

The textual notes show all revisions in "La Gazzetta" (*LG*) and all substantive differences from the *Imperial Magazine* (*IM*) text; my copy-text is the revised "La Gazzetta" (except for line 18, "o'er"). Angle brackets enclose cancellations. I use Bolling's copy of the *Imperial Magazine* at the Huntington Library, where he corrected the epigraph in two places, annotated "Delia" in line 6 as "Nancy Miller," and signed the poem between the epigraph and first line "By R. Bolling jun." Unless otherwise noted, the reading following the closing bracket is from *IM*.

Title The Dove] To a TURTLE-DOVE.
Epigraph
  Tempore] *Bolling crossed out "Tem" at the end of the first line of the IM text,*
    indicating it should start the second line. Contrary to his usual practice,
    Bolling did not write the epigraph in italics in "La Gazzetta," but it is
    printed in italics in IM, and I print it in italics above.
  coissent] woissent [*corrected by Bolling to* coissent]
  Sed] fed [*corrected by Bolling to* Sed]
3 Those] The
4 Depress] Oppress
4 lovelorn] tortur'd
5 Excite such] ⟨Stamp⟩ Excite such ⟨an⟩ *LG*] Stamp such an *IM*
6 Delia] *Bolling added a symbol and the name* Nancy Miller *in the margin of IM*
9 plaintive] ⟨pensive⟩ plaintive *LG*] pensive *IM*
10 Such] Those
11 with] in
16 ne'er seen] unseen
18 o'er] oer *H, LG*] o'er *IM*
22–23 *Replace the following canceled lines in LG*] To ⟨part⟩ break the warmest, tenderest Tyes, / And Vows oft witnessed by the Skies.] *No comparable lines in IM.*
24 Those] *Written over from* These *in LG*] These *IM*
24 killing] bitter
25 those] *written over from* these *in LG*] these *IM*
27 Reptile] insect
28 just Rage] thyself
29 his] its
30 Thus a clear] A limpid
32 Sound] Sound⟨s⟩ *LG*
32 No . . . invade;] If any sound invades the ear,

33   Unless . . . Glade]   At most, a rippling you will hear:
36   It's . . . Eyes:]   The eye with painful terror sees,
37   The . . . terrifies.]   And jarring sounds the ear displease.

14. "Letter to Jerman Baker"

The only extant text is in "La Gazzetta." I have added an apostrophe in "Nancy's" in line 58. Bolling's canceled word(s) follow the closing bracket.

13–15   *A brace on the right brackets these lines.*
17   Was but a dull attempt to]   Coud but be called half-witted
28   disburse]   would give
32–43   *Added at end of poem and marked for insertion here.*
46   as much as you]   and so do you
48–49   *Inserted between lines 47 and 50.*
51   can't so clearly]   cannot wholly
53   steal]   *Four? letters heavily crossed out* take
53   Girl]   Fair
56   *Inserted before this line and then crossed out*   What Lover can such a Jackdaw's bear?
57   But . . . bear?]   But *their* Crow's Voices who can bear?
58–59   *Inserted in the margin.*
65   swarthy]   f__i__fed *One canceled letter after the initial* f *and two or three after the* i *cannot be deciphered.*

15. "The Exile"

The poem is found in "Hilarodiana," and in "La Gazzetta" (the copy-text). Readings from "Hilarodiana" follow the closing bracket. The epigraph is added at the end of the poem, with a note after the title saying "(See the Motto at the End)."

Title   Dated 1762 *in H.*
Epigraph in H   Sine me Liber ibis in Urbim. Ovid.
4   Test]   Jest
5   wretched]   woeful
6   W——]   whore
10   on]   near
10   Getic]   Euxine
11–12   Twou'd . . . there.]   The Cause why he was banish'd there / Might in some Measure sooth his care.
15   please]   sooth
16   a]   one
20   At . . . of]   A Sort of solitary

28–29 *Between these lines, H has* and such like stuff which I postponed / Nine Times in Ten to being alone.
30 He . . . slain] [my?] rugged Guest is gone afar
31 plaintive] Thee friend
44–46 And . . . know] ⟨She Things to you were always kind / I cannot ours call Women—no— / They're female that sometimes may do.⟩
53 Torment] ⟨Bane—soft⟩

16. "The Departure"

There are two texts: in "Hilarodiana," and, revised, in "La Gazzetta" (the copy-text). To the copy-text I have added the stanza divisions found in "Hilarodiana." The following accidentals are also added from "Hilarodiana": commas in lines 9, 10, 11, 13, 26, 27, 41, and 42; a semicolon in line 14; periods at the ends of lines 12, 28, 44, 46, and 54; and parentheses in lines 33 and 41–42. I have emended the poem by adding a semicolon at the end of line 37 and periods at the end of lines 36 and 38.

37 appear'd my Anguish] my Pain suspended
38 *canceled line* And there our Souls were blended. *two draft lines canceled* And there—how we did languish / There Soul with Soul did languish
51–52 *Bolling's note* So in the original and well enough for an Ecclesiastic but for me I prefer "Reflect when thus enchanted / How much the Boon I'd prize." having made no Vows to God that my Portion of Man-hood shall rave without an Object nor think it reasonable to condemn it Tentigine sumpi.
Beside stanzas 3–4 (ll. 17–32) *Drafts written sideways in the inner margin. The Italian is from the last two lines of the second stanza of "La Partenza."*

And you no Thought may lose
(Alas! who knows) on me.
And you no Thought—(O Pain!)
May entertain of me

E tu che sa se mai
Ti sovverai di me
And thou who knows if ever
will think of me

⟨And you who knows O Pain
You'll neer disdain⟩
And you who can decide

May still deride my Sighs
And you ⟨no⟩ a Thought (who knows?)
May never lose on me
And you may never more
In Mind pass o'er my Sighs.
To muse
To ruminate
   meditate

17. "The Angry Lover"

The two texts exist in "Hilarodiana," and, revised, in "La Gazzetta" (the copy-text). To the copy-text I have added the stanza divisions found in "Hilarodiana." The following changes in accidentals are also added from "Hilarodiana": lines 5 and 53, parentheses; line 89, semicolon; and line 97, comma. I have emended the text by adding a semicolon at the end of line 98.

4   have deignd] bestow
48 Silence] Stillness
50 ⟨You still methinks are pretty⟩
51 ⟨Serene—genteel nay—witty⟩
90 Self Pleasure:] I speak; but
91 Heed I] Regard
96 ⟨If e'er occurs my Name.⟩
97–104 ⟨I leave an airy Rover

      You lose a Heart none plainer   You lose a Heart most candid
      Which of us in the Gainer   Whose Fate by this is mended
      Let prudent Nice say
      I know so true a Lover
      No fortune can supply you
      Inconstants that outvie you
      Are th' offer of each Day.⟩
104 A Jill] a jill

Biographical and Geographical Glossary

Note: Names of persons and places within the text that are printed in capitals have their own entries. Full citations are given in the Bibliography for the articles and books noted in short form here; but for brief references to information published in journals, I have adopted the abbreviations used by E. G. Swem in his *Virginia Historical Index* and, for brief references to newspapers, the abbreviations used by Cappon and Duff in the *Virginia Gazette Index*. RB: Robert Bolling, Jr. (1738–1775).

ATKINSON, ROGER (1725–1784), at whose home on Aug. 19 JERMAN BAKER spoke to ANNE MILLER about RB's courtship, lived at Mansfield, near Petersburg, Dinwiddie Co. A merchant and planter, Atkinson, born June 25, 1725, was the son of Roger and Jane Benson Atkinson, of Whitehaven, Cumberland Co., England (Morrison). He emigrated before 1749 (Valentine, 2:6) to the Petersburg area and on April 21, 1753, married Anne, daughter of John Pleasants of Curles, Henrico Co. Two years later Anne Atkinson apologized for not marrying in the Quaker faith and was readmitted to the Society of Friends on "6th 7 mo 1755" (ibid., 2:1207–8). William Senhouse, who visited Virginia in the summer of 1755 as a boy of fifteen, recorded years later that "I was sent ashore by the Captain to the Store of Mr. Roger Atkinson at Petersburg, a few miles from City Point, where our Ship lay, and was civilly treated by him and his Wife, who were opulent Quakers" (Brandow, 30–31). On Dec. 8, 1760, Atkinson was appointed to the vestry of Bristol Parish "in the Room of Mr. HUGH MILLER who is remov'd" and served until he resigned on Nov. 1, 1784, shortly before his death (Chamberlayne, 175–269). When Petersburg was enlarged in 1762, Atkinson, ROBERT BOLLING (1730–1775), and John Banister were made trustees of the town. Atkinson signed the Nonimportation Association agreement of June 22, 1770 (*Rev. Va.*, 1:83). Lewis Burwell recorded that Atkinson shipped fifty hogsheads of tobacco to Great Britain in 1774 and forty-seven hogsheads in 1775 (Thomson, 406). Atkinson built Olive Hill, Chesterfield Co., for his son and namesake Roger Pleasants Atkinson, who was among the one hundred wealthiest Virginians in the late 1780s (Main, 369). Atkinson's letter book, 1769–76, and account book, 1762–89, survive at the University of Virginia Library. A copy of his will, dated Nov. 16, 1782, is in the American Loyalist

Claims, PRO, T 79/17, f. 6. Slaughter (123, 137–40) and Burwell (18–19) list his descendants.

BADWINGTON, where RB on Saturday, Jan. 12, "gave Way to the Impulses of my Passion," was identified by RB as "the Seat of ROBERT BOLLING Esq." Thus Badwington was evidently the name for the early Bolling dwelling in Petersburg. The historian of the later structure, Bollingbrook, writes: "It is generally said that the first Bolling residence in this neighborhood was somewhat further from the Appomattox than East Hill. Some are so specific as to state the original homestead stood near the corner of modern Wythe and Adams Streets" (Voorhis, 549). Petersburg would be a logical place to start on a trip to Sappony River. The Sappony road runs south by southeast from Petersburg across Monks' Neck Creek (just above its juncture with Hatcher Run), across Stony Creek, and to the top of Sappony Creek (Fry and Jefferson map).

BAIRD, JOHN (fl. 1750–76), was a merchant and an attorney of Blandford, Prince George Co. ANNE MILLER was inoculated at his home in Blandford, in March or early April 1760, and told him on Sept. 9 "to acquaint Mr. Johnson that she cou'd no more consider him but as an Enemy." Baird acted as an attorney for HUGH MILLER in 1752 (*VG*27Oct52:22) and in 1760 (*Va. Geneal.* 18:107). On Dec. 11, 1759, he purchased lots nos. 8 and 9 from Hugh Miller for £200 (Weisiger, 74). In 1762 he was, with ROBERT BOLLING (1730–1775) of Bollingbrook, a director and trustee of Blandford (Hening, 7:608–9). William McWhann and Peter Poythress were his partners in the mercantile house of John Baird & Co. Although he was appointed to the Prince George Co. committee of intelligence on May 8, 1775 (along with Richard Bland, Jr., and THEODORICK BLAND, Jr. [*Rev. Va.*, 3:106]), he sympathized with the Loyalists and returned to Scotland in July 1776 (*ibid.*, 4:307, 309n.2). On July 3, 1779, the *Virginia Gazette* reported the death of "Mrs. Jane Baird, wife of John Baird, Esq., of Greencroft, after a long illness" (DN*VG*3Jl79:22).

BAKER, JERMAN (c.1735–1792), RB's advocate with ANNE MILLER, was a lawyer and planter of Chesterfield Co. Best known for his thoughtful letter of Feb. 15, 1764, on Virginia paper currency (12W(1)237–42), he was a member of the grand jury that on Oct. 17, 1766, dismissed the libel charge brought against RB by Col. William Byrd III (*Md. Gaz.* 30Oct66:21). Writing of the bailment of Col. John Chiswell, RB characterized Baker as his "intimate and belov'd Friend" (Lemay, "Bailment," 139). In addition to the "Letter in Answer to One Received from Jerman Baker Esqr—May 1762" (poem no. 14), RB addressed "A Canzonet on a Disappointment" to Baker ("Hilarodiana," 60), a poem expressing regret that Baker had not arrived for a promised visit.

In 1766 John Wayles (1715–1773), as agent for an English tobacco firm, cast aspersions on Baker (Hemphill, 305), but Wayles at this time regarded Baker as a personal enemy (Lemay, "Bailment," 132–33 n.49). He may be the same Jerman Baker who had seven tithes and two chairs in James City Co. in 1768 (*Va. Geneal.* 1:19). On June 22, 1770, Baker signed the Nonimportation Association agreement of burgesses and merchants (*Rev. Va.*, 1:83). Several of his letters are in the Norton Papers at Colonial Williamsburg's Research Department, and he was recorded as a debtor to John Norton & Sons in lists of July 31, 1770, and July 30, 1773 (*Va. Geneal.* 12:78). He married the widow of "the late Mr. James Murray, of Prince George Co." at the beginning of 1773 (PD*VG* 7Jan73:31). As "Clerk to the Meeting," he signed the radical Chesterfield Co. resolves of July 14, 1774 (*Rev. Va.*, 1:118). Lewis Burwell recorded that he shipped thirty hogsheads of tobacco to Great Britain in 1773, eight in 1774, and nine in 1775 (Thomson, 407). Thomas Jefferson wrote him on June 26, 1778, concerning John Wayles's debt to Farrell and Jones (Jefferson, 15:670–71). He served as clerk of the Chesterfield Co. committee of correspondence (*Rev. Va.*, 2:176) and as a delegate from Chesterfield to the House of Delegates of 1779 (Leonard, 133). In that year ROGER ATKINSON wrote: "He thrives apace—has 3 fine children and is in high estimation" (15V359).

Baker settled the complicated estate of William Byrd III and gradually emerged as a leading lawyer of the day. On Feb. 4, 1785, he and Thomson Mason signed John Carr's "License to practice as an attorney in the county of Albemarle and other inferior courts" (Carr Family Papers, Univ. of Va. Library). On March 21, 1786, he witnessed the will of Richard Randolph of Curles who made Baker a guardian of his children (Valentine, 3:1456–59). In his will THEODORICK BLAND, Jr., made Baker one of the trustees of a bequest of land to be used for a college (Weisiger, 137). Baker died on Aug. 31, 1792, at his seat Archers Hill in Chesterfield Co. (*Va. Gaz. & Gen. Advertiser*, Sept. 5, 1792, p. 3). His will, dated 1792, and invoice are in the Chesterfield Co. Will Book 4:497–501, 512–28 (Va. State Library and Archives).

BEVERLEY, HARRY (c.1732–1773), planter, of Hazelwood, Caroline Co., whom RB made the speaker of the revised version of his poem "The Dupe" (poem no. 6), was the son of Robert Beverley (1701–1733) and Ann Stanard Beverley of Newlands, Spotsylvania Co., and the grandson of Capt. Harry Beverley (c.1670–1730). Stanard says Beverley entered the College of William and Mary in 1756 (20V437). About 1762 he married LUCY ROY, daughter of Thomas and Judith Beverley Roy. Lucy was his first cousin. She died shortly after the marriage (Warren, 187). In 1765 he married, second, JANE WILEY ROY (Warner, 203), Lucy's first cousin (but no relation to him). They had several children.

BEVERLEY, ROBERT (1740–1800), planter, of Blandfield, Essex Co., the likely addressee of "A Circumstantial Account," was RB's old school chum, still in England until after 1760. He was the grandson of Robert Beverley (c. 1673–1722), the historian, and the son of William Beverley (c. 1698–1756) and Elizabeth Bland Beverley (McGill, 534) of Blandfield, Essex Co. Born Aug. 21, 1740 (34V162), he entered the Wakefield Grammar School, England, in 1750 (Beverley, "Diary"), a year before RB. Beverley remained in England when RB returned to Virginia in 1755. He entered the Middle Temple, Jan. 5, 1757; matriculated at Trinity College, Cambridge, May 19, 1757 (*Alumni Cantabrigiensis*, pt. 2, 1:254); and was called to the bar Feb. 6, 1761 (Jones, 20). On Feb. 3, 1763, he married Maria, the daughter of Landon and Maria Byrd Carter (34V162; McGill, 535). By 1775, when RB—a committed patriot— died, Beverley was known as a conservative tinged with loyalism. In the 1780s he was among the one hundred wealthiest men in Virginia (Main, 369). Robert Hunter, Jr., recorded the festivities at Blandford on Dec. 1–4, 1785, when Beverley's daughter Maria married Richard Randolph, Jr., of Curles (Hunter, 206–9). Beverley died at Blandfield on April 12, 1800 (*Va. Gaz. & Gen. Advertiser*, April 18, 1800, p. 3).

BLACK, WILLIAM (1720–1782), who told RB at MURRAY'S on Sept. 13, 1760, that HUGH MILLER had ordered his children to FLOWER-DE-HUNDRED to prepare for sailing, was a merchant, planter, and unscrupulous entrepreneur of Manchester (now South Richmond), Chesterfield Co. He kept a diary while acting as secretary to the Virginia commissioners at the Lancaster Treaty with the Iroquois in 1744 (Black; Kagle, 85–86). He may be the William Black who married Ann Dent of Overwharton Parish on Oct. 17, 1745 (Wulfeck, ser. 1, 1:120). On Feb. 7, 1760, he witnessed a deed in Prince George Co. (Weisiger, 76). The third owner of the famous thoroughbred horse Ranter (35V368), he is probably the same William Black who served as a justice of the peace of King and Queen Co., beginning Oct. 17, 1772 (McIlwaine, 117). He acquired the principal estate of Speaker John Robinson and one of Bernard Moore's plantations and sold them to George Washington in 1773. On Dec. 6, 1773, Washington wrote in disgust: "Was there ever such a Man as Black! Crafty and designing, and yet so stupidly ignorant and negligent in so important a matter as this!" (*Writings*, 37:504). Mary Willing Byrd, the widow of William Byrd III, wrote JERMAN BAKER on Dec. 4, 1781, complaining of "that wretch Black" who acquired Falls Plantation, Chesterfield Co., from her husband's estate (Va. Hist. Soc. MS). Black's death was announced in the *Va. Gaz. and Weekly Advertiser* on Feb. 2, 1782, p. 3. His will was proved in Chesterfield Co. in 1782 (22W(1)133).

BLAND, JOHN (1741–1794), merchant, of Petersburg, and Blandford. Although there were numerous John Blands, the one who visited London in 1759 is probably the person who reported to RB the rumor of THEODORICK BLAND's marriage to ANNE MILLER. He was the son of John Bland (1712–1787) of Lime Street, London (Joseph Hunter 2:427). He signed the Nonimportation Resolution of June 22, 1770 (Jefferson, 1:47). Lewis Burwell recorded that he shipped 167 hogsheads of tobacco to England in 1773 and 248 in 1774 (Thomson, 406).

BLAND, THEODORICK, Jr. (1742–1790), who in 1762–63 was rumored to have married ANNE MILLER, was a physician, planter, cavalry officer, and politician of Cawsons, near the mouth of Appomattox River, Prince George Co. (Bolling, *Memoir*, 46–47). He and RB were schoolfellows at Wakefield and later became close friends. At the end of his poem "The House Moving," dated Aug. 1767, RB noted: "Dr. Bland who abhors Rhyme advised me to write something in Blank Verse. I know that every little Poetaster cou'd rhyme & therefore was unwilling to engage in an Enterprize which demands very great Talents, Mediocrity being insufferable in that Species of Poetry. At Length however I writ the Housemoving—a mean Subject meanly treated. Therefore the Doctor was a Coquin for his Advice & myself for taking it an egregious Ignoramus" ("La Gazzetta," 84). RB made Bland his executor. We know from an account by "Observator" (whom I believe to be Pierre Etienne Du Ponceau) that Bland intended in 1788 to publish a collection of RB's poetry ([Du Ponceau], 211–13).

Bland was born March 21, 1741/42 and baptized April 26, 1742 (Chamberlayne, 291, cf. 288). He was the son of Theodorick Bland (1719–1784) of Cawsons and Frances Bolling Bland (1742–1774). His mother was the daughter of Drury Bolling and the granddaughter of Col. Robert Bolling (1646–1709), the emigrant, and Anne Stith Bolling; Theodorick Bland was thus the half second cousin of RB and the second cousin of Anne Miller. The statesman Richard Bland (1710–1776), who became, about 1762, RB's stepfather, was his uncle. After attending school at Wakefield (he left in 1759), Bland studied medicine at Edinburgh and took an M.D. there in 1763 (*List*, 8). He courted Anne Miller in 1761–62. Still in Edinburgh when PEYTON SKIPWITH came to Scotland to woo her (Campbell, 23–26), he returned to Virginia in 1764. On Oct. 14, 1765, he was elected to the Bristol Parish vestry and served until his resignation on Feb. 1, 1779 (Chamberlayne, 202–60 passim). About 1768 he married MARTHA DANGERFIELD (evidently the "fair Dangerfield" of poem no. 14).

On April 17, 1771, Bland was added to the Prince George Co. list of justices of the peace (*Exec. Journals*, 6:402). In June 1774 he was clerk of the meeting of the Prince George Co. inhabitants who directed their representatives to oppose the English. On May 8, 1775, he served on the Prince George Committee of Correspondence. He helped remove the arms from the governor's residence in Williamsburg to the powder magazine on June 24, 1775. Writing under the pseudonym "Cassius," he attacked Lord Dunmore and the Scottish traders in Virginia in the newspapers (*Rev. Va.*, 1:152, 3:106, 4:114—15 [reprinting *PVG* 15S75]).

On June 14, 1776, he was appointed captain of the 1st Troop of Virginia Cavalry and advertised for horses in the newspapers on July 5. On Dec. 4 he was promoted to major of the Light Dragoons; and on March 31, 1777, he became colonel of the 1st Regiment of Continental Light Dragoons (Sanchez-Saavedra, 101—2). He commanded cavalry in the battles of Wilmington on July 23, 1777, and the battle of the Brandywine on Sept. 11, 1777. On Nov. 5, 1778, Washington charged Bland with escorting Burgoyne's defeated Convention Army from Connecticut to Virginia. When his military duties allowed, he served in the Virginia assembly as a senator (1776, 1777—78, and 1778; Leonard, 124, 127, 131). He asked Jefferson on June 14, 1779, if he could rent Monticello while Jefferson, as governor of Virginia, lived in Williamsburg (Jefferson, 2:291—92). After Bland resigned from the service in Aug. 1779 (Sanchez-Saavedra, 119), he retired to his plantation, Farmingdale (or Kippax), Prince George Co. Gov. Patrick Henry appointed him colonel of the Prince George Co. Militia in 1785. In 1786, when he unsuccessfully opposed Edmund Randolph for the governorship, he was among the one hundred wealthiest men in Virginia (Main, 370). He served in the Virginia House of Delegates for 1786—87, 1787—88, and 1788, as well as in the Virginia convention of 1788 where he voted against adopting the U.S. Constitution (Leonard, 162, 166, 170, and 174). In 1788 he was elected to the first U.S. House of Representatives and served from March 4, 1789, to his death on June 1, 1790, in New York where Congress was in session. His will was dated Nov. 5, 1789, and recorded Aug. 12, 1790 (abstract in Weisiger, 137).

BLANDFORD, Prince George Co., where ANNE MILLER and ELIZA-BETH STARKE made a ball on Feb. 13 and where Anne Miller was inoculated at BAIRD's, was a town on the south side of the Appomattox River, just below Petersburg (*see* RB's map). It is now part of Petersburg.

BOLLING, Col. ALEXANDER (1721/22—1767), who agreed to ANNE MILLER's request on Sept. 9, 1760, to remind HUGH MILLER of "the difficulties he had to encounter in his Addresses to my Mother," was a planter and burgess who lived at MITCHELS, on the Appomattox, Prince George Co. He was born March 12, 1721/22, the son of Stith and Elizabeth (widow of John Hartwell) Bolling. On Dec. 23, 1745, he married his first cousin SUSANNA BOLLING (1728—post 1773). On March 4, 1745/46, he and JAMES MUR-

RAY were appointed justices of the peace of Prince George Co., but on April 30, 1752, in restructuring the courts, the Council left him out of the commission, as it did again on June 15, 1753. Then on June 8, 1757, the Council ordered him added "to the Quorum" along with Murray. (*Exec. Journals*, 5:199, 394, 436, 6:51.) On April 3, 1746, he was appointed one of three coroners for the county (ibid., 5:205).

On Nov. 6, 1749, he was elected to the Bristol Parish vestry. He served as a churchwarden from March 1, 1750/51, to Nov. 20, 1752 (Chamberlayne, 135–88). On June 22, 1752, the vestry minutes recorded that "James Murray, Alexander Bolling, & Theodoric Bland [Sr.] are permitted to Build a Gallery in the South End of the addition to be made to the Church at their Own Expence; for the use of themselves and Families and their Heirs and Successors" (ibid., 146). He was elected a burgess from Prince George Co. in the assemblies of 1756–58, 1758–61, and 1766–68 (Leonard, 87, 89, 96). He died June 11, 1767.

BOLLING (later Bland), ELIZABETH BLAIR (c. 1710–1775), RB's mother, who, according to Bolling Stark's letter of Sept. 7, 1760, in the "Circumstantial Account," could not be reconciled to RB's "leaving her" and going to Scotland with the Millers. She was the daughter of Dr. Archibald Blair (c. 1665–1733) and Sarah Archer Fowler Blair, the widow of Bartholomew Fowler. She was thus the niece of Dr. James Blair (1655–1743), founder and president of the College of William and Mary (Parke Rouse, 7, 177, 268; *DAB*), and half sister of John Blair (1687–1771) who was acting governor of Virginia four times from 1758 to 1768. She married (as his second wife) Col. John Bolling (1700–1757) of COBBS, Chesterfield Co., on Aug. 1, 1728. RB recorded that they had "many children, some of whom died in their infancy," and listed eight children who survived, including his sister MARY BOLLING (*Memoir*, 5). After John Bolling's death, on Sept. 5, 1757, she continued to live at Cobbs until her marriage to Richard Bland (1710–1776; *DAB*), the statesman, which evidently took place about 1762 or 1763. RB's first wife died at Jordan's, Bland's plantation in Prince George Co., on May 2, 1764; RB's mother had evidently married and taken up residence at Bland's before then. Purdie's *Virginia Gazette* of April 28, 1775, announced the death of "Mrs. Elizabeth Bland, spouse to Col. Richard Bland, of Jordan's, in Prince George; a Lady not more distinguished by her good sense and sweetness of temper, than for the many virtues which adorned her character through life."

BOLLING (later Bland), MARY (1744–1775), the eldest of RB's three young sisters (Sarah was born in 1748, and Anne was born in 1752), was evidently the sister present at BROADWAY with RB, ANNE MILLER, and others on Jan.

31, 1760, when RB, "without much violence," brought Anne Miller back to COBBS. She was inoculated with MARY HERBERT CLAIBORNE and others on June 2, 1760, at IRELAND. On Oct. 8, 1761, she married Richard Bland, Jr. (Feb. 20, 1730/31–post 1765), of Jordan's, Prince George Co. Bland joined his father as a burgess from Prince George Co. in the assembly of 1761–65 (Leonard, 93). About a year after Mary's marriage, her mother ELIZABETH BLAIR BOLLING, the widow of Col. John Bolling (1700–1757), married the elder Richard Bland (1710–1776), statesman. Robertson lists Mary's children as Richard Bland (1762–1806) and Ann P. Bland (b. 1765) (Wyndham Robertson, 36). The genealogical chart of the Bland family, copied for John Randolph of Roanoke about 1825 (Va. Hist. Soc. MS), names four children: Richard Bland, William B. Bland, Eliza Bland, and Ann Poythress Bland.

BOLLING, Col. ROBERT (1730–1775), planter and merchant of BADWINGTON and, later, Bollingbrook (in present-day Petersburg), Dinwiddie Co., was ANNE MILLER's uncle and RB's half first cousin once removed. To distinguish himself from this older cousin, RB customarily appended "jun." or "of Chellow" after his name. On Jan. 12, 1760, RB became intoxicated at Badwington and amazed his friends by declaring his love for Anne Miller and by repeatedly kissing her. Col. Robert Bolling of Bollingbrook was the youngest of eight children (and the only son) of Robert Bolling (1682–1749) and Anne Meriwether Bolling. Three of his older sisters (MARY BOLLING STARKE, JANE BOLLING MILLER, and SUSANNA BOLLING BOLLING) figure in RB's "Account." He represented Dinwiddie Co. as a burgess in the assemblies of 1756–58, 1761–65, 1766–68, 1769, 1772–74, 1775–76, and in the First Convention of 1774 (Leonard, 86, 91, 94, 97, 102, 105, 110; Rev. Va., 1:122, 220). He signed the Nonimportation Resolutions of May 18, 1769, and the Convention Association of Aug. 6, 1774 (Rev. Va., 1:76, 235). He was appointed a vestryman of Bristol Parish on Jan. 5, 1760, served as churchwarden for a year beginning on Nov. 13, 1767, and resigned on April 23, 1770 (Chamberlayne, 172, 213, 221). Colonel of the militia of Dinwiddie Co., he also served as a justice of the peace, appearing third in the lists of Aug. 1, 1763, Aug. 16, 1765, and Nov. 24, 1766; and second in the lists of Nov. 17, 1769, July 17, 1771, and Nov. 6, 1771 (McIlwaine, 64, 68[2], 75, 95, 111, 112). He married, first, Martha Banister, sister of Col. John Banister of Battersea, and, second, on April 11, 1758, Mary Marshall Tabb (d. 1814), daughter of Col. Thomas Tabb, of Clay Hill, Amelia Co. (4V331). Their son Robert Bolling (1759–1839) of Center Hill married RB's daughter Mary Burton Bolling (1764–1787) on Nov. 4, 1781.

BOLLING, ROBERT, Jr. (1738–1775), of CHELLOW, BUCKINGHAM Co. See Introduction.

BOLLING, SUSANNA BOLLING (1728–post 1773), the daughter of Robert and Anne Meriwether Bolling, was born June 16, 1728. She was the sister of MARY BOLLING STARKE, JANE BOLLING MILLER, and ROBERT BOLLING (1730–1775), and the aunt of ANNE MILLER. She married her first cousin ALEXANDER BOLLING on Dec. 23, 1745. They lived at MITCHELS, Prince George Co., and had eight children, whose births, along with other family vital statistics, are recorded in the Bible that the Rev. Samuel Davies gave her "as a small token of gratitude for her kindness" (Warfield).

Because ROGER ATKINSON wrote BENSON FIERON on June 11, 1773, that he has received money from Susanna Bolling for Fieron, I assume she lived until sometime thereafter.

BROADWAY, where RB saw ANNE MILLER on Jan. 24 and Aug. 25, 1760, was the home of MARY BOLLING STARKE. RB located it on the south side of the Appomattox River, Prince George Co., about halfway between Petersburg and the junction of the Appomattox and James rivers (*see* RB's map). In 1781 Jefferson reported that Gen. William Smallwood engaged in a skirmish at Broadway's (Jefferson 4:399).

BROOKS, "SUKY" (fl. 1760), HUGH MILLER's housekeeper. Unidentified.

BUCKINGHAM COUNTY, the site of RB's primary estate, CHELLOW(E), was created out of Albemarle Co. in 1761. It was coterminous with Tillotson Parish. It is south of Charlottesville and west of Richmond. Almost all of its records were burned in a fire in 1859. (Dorman; Whitley.)

BURTON (later Bolling), MARY ("Polly") (c.1747–1764), RB's first wife, was the daughter of William Burton III (fl. 1731–1770) of the Old Plantation, Northampton Co. Among RB's poems addressed to her are "On a Finally Happy Lover," dated from "Warm-Springs in Aug[ust]a, July, 1762"; his "Canzonet of Chiabrera Imitated" (beginning "Polly Burton's Hair flows down"), a revision of a poem originally about ANNE MILLER (poem no. 3); and his "Epistle to Miss M. Burton," dated "Chellowe," Jan. 1, 1763 ("La Gazzetta," 8, 5–7). Their marriage license bond was recorded in Northampton Co. on June 3, 1763 (Nottingham, 9). As RB said in the "Account," they were married at the Old Plantation on June 5, 1763. The next day, RB wrote a poem "To My Wife" celebrating their happiness (*London Magazine* 33 [Jan. 1764]: 44–45; Lemay, *Calendar*, no. 1954). She died "in Child-Bed" two days after the birth of her daughter, Mary Burton Bolling (1764–1787), at Jordan's, May 2, 1764. When Mary's sister, Margaret Burton (d. 1772), married Littleton Savage, the newspapers noted she had a fortune of "at least" £10,000 (*RVG* 4F68:22). RB's "Funeral Oration to the Memory of Mrs. Mary Bolling," dated "Jordans, May 15, 1764," is in his manuscript volume "A Collection" (36–45). A nineteenth-century copy (revised, so it may reflect a version revised by RB), entitled "A Pathetic Soliloquy," is in the Library of Congress. RB's brief "Madrigal, Attributed to Abbé Chaulieu, Imitated, in Memory of Mrs. M. Bolling," appeared in the *London Magazine* 33 (Sept. 1764): 478 (Lemay, *Calendar*, no. 2000); the two following poems in the *London Magazine* (Lemay, *Calendar*, nos. 1998 and 2001) evidently also lament her death. "The Air from Metastasio" (no. 2001) was reprinted "Set to Music by W. Atkinson, of Lincoln," in the *London Magazine* 33 (Dec. 1764): 651 (Lemay, *Calendar*, no. 2012).

Because Margaret and Littleton Savage had no children, Bolling's daughter Mary Burton Bolling inherited the entire estate of William Burton III (Whitelaw, 144). She married Robert Bolling (1759–1839) of Center Hill, son of Col. ROBERT BOLLING (1730–1775) and Mary Marshall Tabb Bolling.

CALLAN, Mr. (fl. 1762), who informed RB on May 9, 1762, of HUGH MILLER's death in London, was probably an English merchant or a ship captain.

CHARLES CITY COUNTY, one of the eight original Virginia shires formed in 1634, is on the north side of the James River, across from Prince George Co. (*see* RB's map).

CHELLOW (often Chellowe), RB's plantation in BUCKINGHAM Co., is now called Indian Gap, off county rt. 623, south of Sprouses Corner. RB named it for the Bolling ancestral home in England, near Ilkley, which was owned by a distant cousin, Elizabeth Bolling, who befriended RB when he was a student (Bolling, *Memoir*, 9). He moved there from COBBS in 1760, built a larger house on a higher hill in Aug. 1767, and drew a sketch of it to accompany his poem "The House Moving" ("La Gazzetta," 79–84; sketch on p. 84). He added a separate library in 1772 ("La Gazzetta," i).

CHESTERFIELD COUNTY, created out of Henrico Co. in 1748, is on the north side of the Appomattox River, across from parts of Amelia, Dinwiddie, and Prince George counties. The Bolling family home COBBS was in Chesterfield Co. (*see* RB's map; Odell).

CLAIBORNE (later Harrison), MARY HERBERT ("Roxana") (1744/45–ante 1787), who "had a fine shape, some Sense and more Beauty," was inoculated with MARY BOLLING and others at Ireland on June 2, 1760, and flirted with RB on June 6, 1760. She was the daughter of Col. Augustine Claiborne (1721–1789) and Mary Herbert Claiborne of Windsor, Sussex Co. (Slaughter, 167). Augustine Claiborne mentioned eight sons, Herbert, Augustine, Buller,

William, John, Thomas, Richard, and Bathurst, in his will, and one of them was inoculated with "Roxana." In 1761 she married Charles Harrison, the brother of CARTER HENRY HARRISON and later a general. She may be the same Mary Harrison who, on Aug. 9, 1774, wrote ROGER ATKINSON calling for repayment of a loan. Atkinson wrote Samuel Pleasants, Feb. 24, 1775, that he would repay her "after our General Court at Wmsburg," but on June 3, 1775, he confessed that "the total stop put to . . . everythin here . . . by the Embarassment of public Affairs, hath wholly disconcerted me" (Atkinson letter book and account book, Univ. of Va. Library). In his will, made on May 1, 1787, Augustine Claiborne mentioned his "daughter Harrison dec'd" (Claiborne Family Papers, Va. Hist. Soc.).

COBBS, where RB was carried away by his emotions for ANNE MILLER after "a little Entertainment" on Feb. 26, 1760, was the primary Bolling family seat in the first half of the eighteenth century. It was in CHESTERFIELD Co., on the north side of the Appomattox River about three miles above its juncture with the James River. John Bolling I (1676–1729), RB's grandfather, purchased the Cobbs tract of land in 1704 and built a home there within the decade. William Byrd of Westover visited Cobbs on his way back from the dividing line expedition in 1728 (*Prose Works*, 319).

It was the primary home of John Bolling II (1700–1757), RB's father. RB lived there with his mother from 1758 until he built a house at CHELLOW in mid-1760. William A. Bolling sketched Cobbs as it existed in 1816 (O'Dell, 302); it was then a three-part house: a two-story central block with two wings of one and a half stories set at right angles to it. Although Jeffrey M. O'Dell suspects that the house may have been built in stages, with part of the structure dating from the late eighteenth century, the history of the occupants shows that it was most fully occupied at two early periods. John Bolling I, who was very wealthy, lived there with his wife and six children in the 1710s and 1720s; his son, John Bolling II, also quite wealthy, lived there with his wife and eight children in the 1740s and 1750s. Because RB celebrated "old" Cobbs in a 1760s poem ("La Gazzetta," 92–97), I suspect that most or all of the building was erected c. 1710. The property was sold out of the family in 1827 (43V346) and was burned by Federal troops in 1864 (John Robertson, 9).

DALGLEISH, Dr. JOHN (d. 1771), who appraised the estate of JOHN HERBERT with RB and JAMES MILNER on July 15, 1760 (the inventory is printed in 18V189), later practiced medicine at Norfolk. An authority on inoculation, he was involved in the Norfolk anti-inoculation riots. He published an account of his experiences in the *Supplement* to Rind's *Va. Gaz.*, Aug. 25, 1768, and followed it up with two more articles, Nov. 2 and 23, 1769 (Rind). RB tried to "turn to Farce" the whole Norfolk affair with his poem "Civil Dudgeon: A

Canzonet" ("A Collection," 75–79). The obituary in Purdie and Dixon's *Va. Gaz.*, Oct. 3, 1771, judged Dalgleish "an honest man as well as a skilful Physician."

DANGERFIELD (or Daingerfield), [MARTHA?]. In his doggerel letter to Jerman Baker (poem no. 14), RB hoped that Dr. THEODORICK BLAND would not marry ANNE MILLER but instead "the fair Dangerfield." Because Bland married Martha Daingerfield (Campbell, xx; *DAB*), the daughter of Edwin and Hannah Bland Daingerfield, I suspect Martha was the "fair Dangerfield." Martha was the sister of Col. William Daingerfield of Belvidera. After Bland's death, she married Patrick Corran. Her will, dated Sept. 24, 1804, is in the Virginia State Library and Archives (Harrower, 174n.25).

DINWIDDIE COUNTY, created out of PRINCE GEORGE Co. in 1752, is on the south side of the Appomattox River, across from CHESTERFIELD Co. (*see* RB's map).

FIERON (or Fearon), BENSON (fl. 1760–89), who was at BROADWAY on Jan. 24, 1760, with RB, ANNE MILLER and ELIZABETH STARKE, was a merchant of London, England, and Petersburg, Virginia. He was the half brother of ROGER ATKINSON (Morrison, 347). A series of letters from Atkinson to Fieron, 1769–1773, survive in Atkinson's letter book, and letters from 1775 to Nov. 16, 1789, are in Atkinson's account book, University of Virginia Library.

FLEMING, WILLIAM (1736?–1824), whom RB identified as the plaintive speaker (and disappointed lover) in "To Stella" (poem no. 12) was a soldier, planter, merchant, lawyer, burgess, congressman, judge, and third president of the Supreme Court of Appeals of Virginia. Son of Col. John Fleming (1697–1756) of Mount Pleasant, Goochland Co. (the site successively became part of Cumberland Co. and finally Powhatan Co.), and of Mary Bolling Fleming (1711–1744), the daughter of John Bolling I (1676–1729) of COBBS, Fleming was RB's first cousin. He is said to have graduated from the College of William and Mary in 1761 or 1763, but both dates are late for someone born in 1736. He served as a burgess from Cumberland Co. in the sessions of 1772–74 and 1775–76, was elected to all five Virginia Conventions in 1774–76, and served as a delegate in the Virginia assembly in 1776 and 1777–78—first from Cumberland and then, upon its formation in 1778, from Powhatan Co. (Leonard, 102, 105, 109, 112, 114, 117, 119, 122, 125).

He married Elizabeth Champe on Oct. 5, 1776 (Stanard, 24V327). His final major elective office was as delegate to the Continental Congress, 1779–81

(*Biographical Directory*, 950). In 1788 he was appointed a judge of the Virginia General Court. Upon the organization of Virginia's Supreme Court of Appeals in 1789, Fleming was elected one of its five judges and became its president in 1809, serving until his death (Mays). He corresponded frequently with his former college chum Thomas Jefferson. In 1796 Benjamin Henry Latrobe wrote that his reputation as a doctor (acquired by treating himself, his family, slaves, and neighbors) was very great (Latrobe, 1:108–9, 2:541). According to the *Lynchburg Virginian*, March 2, 1824, p. 3, Fleming died at Summerville, Chesterfield Co., on Feb. 24, 1824, age ninety.

FLOWER-DE-HUNDRED, a little settlement on the south side of the James River, Prince George Co., where the *Peggy* moored (*see* RB's map), was corrupted by popular etymology from Flowerdew Hundred, one of the seven original particular plantations, or hundreds, which elected burgesses to Virginia's first General Assembly in 1619. Governor George Yeardley named the site for his wife, Temperance Flowerdew. *See* JOHN HOOD.

GLOUCESTER COUNTY, where RB made an excursion in March 1760, was formed in 1651 from York Co. It lies on the north side of the York River, north of Williamsburg.

GRENOCK, HUGH MILLER's primary residence, was in Prince George Co., on the south side of the Appomattox River, about two miles east of Blandford (*see* RB's map).

HARE, Mr., a goldsmith of Pocahontas (incorporated 1752, on the north bank of the Appomattox, opposite Petersburg), CHESTERFIELD Co., from whom RB ordered a wedding ring for ANNE MILLER. He may have been Parker Hare, who lived "near Petersburg" and advertised in May 1769 for a runaway female slave wearing "silver buckles" (RVG 26Oct69:31). (Cutten does not record any goldsmith named Hare.)

HARRISON, CARTER HENRY (1736–1793), who was "discarded" by ELIZABETH STARKE at ROBERT WALKER's on Jan. 14 and who suffered while she and RB played up to one another at BROADWAY on Jan. 31, 1760, was a planter of Clifton, Cumberland Co. Named for his mother's father, Robert "King" Carter of Corotoman, he was the son of Benjamin and Anne Carter Harrison of Berkeley, Charles City Co.; the brother of Benjamin Harrison (1726?–1801), the Signer; and the uncle of President William Henry Harrison. After attending the College of William and Mary, he went to London and was admitted to the Middle Temple on Jan. 1, 1754 (Jones, 96). Returning to Virginia, he served in 1755 as a captain in George Washington's Virginia Regiment but became ill and resigned in December in favor of his brother Henry (Washington, *Papers*, 2:25, 43, 84, 214, 3:21).

He married Susanna Randolph (1738–1806), the daughter of Isham Randolph (1687–1742) of Dungeness, Goochland Co., on Nov. 9, 1760, and they had six children (Cowden, 382–83). He was a justice of the peace for Cumberland Co., listed eleventh on Jan. 17, 1764, and seventh on Nov. 5, 1768 (McIlwaine, 63, 90). John Wayles maligned him with many others in 1766, claiming that in disappointing the ships of those to whom he owed money, Harrison was "acting in Character" (Hemphill, 303). He chaired the Cumberland Co. committee of safety and drafted the instructions adopted on April 22, 1776, directing John Mayo and WILLIAM FLEMING, delegates to the Fifth Virginia Convention, "positively to declare for an Independency; that you solemnly abjure any allegiance to his Britannick Majesty, and bid him a good Night forever" (*Rev. Va.*, 6:433). Harrison served as a delegate from Cumberland Co. to the House of Burgesses in 1772 and to the House of Delegates in 1783, 1785–86, and 1786–87 (Leonard, 145, 149, 153, 156, 160).

In the 1780s he was among the one hundred richest men in Virginia, and the Harrison family was the second wealthiest (after the Carters) in the state (Main, 364, 376). Cowden (383) says he died in Jan. 1794, but Harrison gives the date as 1793.

HAYNES, HERBERT (fl. 1760–71), at whose home on Sappony River on Thursday, Jan. 17, 1760, RB proposed to follow ANNE MILLER to Scotland, is probably the Herbert Haynes who married Sarah Wynne Dalton (15V428). He was a justice of the peace of Dinwiddie Co.: eleventh in the list of Aug. 1, 1763; twelfth, Aug. 16, 1765, and Nov. 24, 1766; and eighth, Nov. 17, 1769, July 17, 1771, and Nov. 6, 1771 (McIlwaine, 68 (2), 76, 95, 111, 112). He may be the Herbert Haynes of Warren Co., N.C., whose inventory (c. 1793) survives in the Bland family papers at the Virginia Historical Society.

HENRICO COUNTY, an original shire formed in 1634, is on the north side of the James River, across from Chesterfield Co. (*see* RB's map).

HERBERT, JOHN (d. 1760). A lawyer and planter of Chesterfield Co., whose estate (and large belletristic library) RB, JOHN DALGLEISH, and JAMES MILNER appraised, was the son of Richard Herbert (d. 1731) and Phebe Herbert. He sold a choice tract of 1,270 acres in Dinwiddie Co., to Sir William Skipwith, father of Sir PEYTON SKIPWITH. He left his estate to his "brother" William Anderson and to Herbert Claiborne, son of his cousin Mary Herbert Claiborne and Augustine Claiborne. He was the uncle of "Roxana," MARY HERBERT CLAIBORNE (18V189–90; 80V53).

HOOD, JOHN (d. 1766), whom RB considered "a Gentleman of Humanity and Honor," was a merchant, shipbuilder, and entrepreneur who sailed with the Millers on the *Peggy*, Captain McLAUGHLIN, for Scotland on Oct. 17, 1760. He lived at Flower-de-Hundred on the James River between Flower de Hundred Creek and Ward's Creek, Prince George Co. When James Rookings, ship carpenter, died in Feb. 1750/51, the uncompleted frame of a scow he was building "on Account of Mr. John Hood" was offered for sale (*VG* 21F51:41). On moving from Williamsburg to Flower-de-Hundred in 1755, Dr. ALEXANDER JAMESON advertised that he was "to be found at the House of Mr. John Hood, at which place an Apothecary's shop will be kept by Robert Arbuthnot" (*VG* 19D55:31). Hood sold JAMES JOHNSON of Martin's Brandon Parish, Prince George Co., a series of tracts containing 760 acres on Jan. 30, 1757 (Weisiger, 78). Hood operated a tobacco warehouse and ferry. Maria Taylor Byrd wrote her son William Byrd III on July 18, 1760, that Hood was returning to England and "designs to see your sons & the Otways." She noted that she was sending duplicates of her son's letters and power of attorney to the Otways by Hood (Tinling, 699).

The site of his home at Flower-de-Hundred was called "Hoods" throughout the Revolution (Jefferson, 3:530, 4:258, 260, etc.; *Rev. Va.*, 6:235 n.5). After his death, his estate advertised his "valuable library of instructive and entertaining books, of the best editions," including Richardson's *Sir Charles Grandison*, Smollett's *History of England*, and Molière's plays in French and English (PD*VG* 20Je66:31).

IRELAND, where MARY HERBERT CLAIBORNE and RB's younger siblings were inoculated on June 2, 1760. Unidentified.

JAMESON, Dr. ALEXANDER (d. 1766), at whose home in Blandford, on Thursday, May 22, 1760, RB had an attack of malaria, was a physician. RB characterized him in Sept. 1764 as a "Dictator upon all Things in his Neighborhood" ("La Gazzetta," 59). Jameson purchased a house in Williamsburg from John Pearson Webb in 1752. In 1755 he moved from Williamsburg to JOHN HOOD's at Flower-de-Hundred, where he also ran an apothecary shop. On Oct. 9, 1759, Dr. Jameson purchased three lots and buildings in Blandford and moved there (Weisiger, 73). Bristol Parish paid him in 1762 for attending Ann West (Chamberlayne, 194). An advertisement for the sale of his Blandford estate appeared in July 1766 (PD*VG* 4Jl66:31). A selection of titles from his library was advertised at his death (4W(1)269).

JOHNSON (or Johnston), JAMES (fl. 1758–89?), whom RB thought "an artful, designing Scoundrel," was the friend and confidant of HUGH MILLER. Johnson was evidently a merchant of Glasgow and Martin's Brandon

Parish, Prince George Co. He purchased 760 acres in the parish from JOHN HOOD on Jan. 30, 1757, and sold them on March 11, 1760, for £800 (Weisiger, 78). In his will Hugh Miller identified Johnson as "late of Glasgow, merchant" (10V323). He may be the James Johnson who, in partnership with Claude Nisbett, sued André Munroe in Oct. 1758 for £24.15.4 and sued Richard Lee in April 1760 for £140 (12V23). On Dec. 11, 1759, he witnessed Hugh Miller's sale to JOHN BAIRD of lot nos. 8 and 9 in Blandford (Weisiger, 74). He is probably the James Johnston, Glasgow merchant, whom George Pottie mentioned to John Norton on Aug. 10, 1775 (Frances Mason, 383). (RB spelled his name "Johnston" in poem no. 14.) He may be the James Johnson who died in Spital Square, London, on July 19, 1789 (*Gentleman's Magazine*, July 1789, p. 673).

McLAUGHLIN, Capt., evidently the captain of the *Peggy*, who was to deliver RB's letter of Sept. 30 to ANNE MILLER after the Millers reached Glasgow. The *Peggy* sailed from FLOWER-DE-HUNDRED for Glasgow on Oct. 17, 1760, taking the Miller family and JOHN HOOD. He is probably the same Captain McLaughlin who was sailing in the 1770s (PD*VG* 24Oct71 : 23).

MILLER, ANNE ("Nancy") (1742/43 – 1779). *See* Introduction.

MILLER (or Millar), HUGH (fl. 1740 – 62). The "barbarous old Harlowe," who insisted on carrying his daughter ANNE MILLER back to Scotland, was a merchant and planter of GRENOCK, near BLANDFORD, PRINCE GEORGE Co. A Scottish merchant from Glasgow, he was in Virginia before 1740. By 1741 he married JANE, the daughter of Robert Bolling (1682 – 1749) and Anne Meriwether Bolling (5W(1)276; cf. 4V330). In the early twentieth century, "a Handsome silver castor," evidently from Miller's family silver, was extant: "owned by Rev. William Munford, of Md., bears a coat, representing Miller impaling Bolling, the former being three wolves' heads erased gu" (6W(1)128).

On March 16, 1741, Hugh Miller visited William Byrd II at Westover, played cards, and had dinner. He visited again with his wife on June 4, dined with other visitors, played bowls after dinner and cards in the evening; after spending the night, they played bowls again after dinner on June 5 and then left. Mrs. Miller and a friend "came from over the river to dinner" on June 24. On Sunday, July 12, Byrd noted that Mrs. Miller "came and dined here but none beside came." Hugh and Jane Miller visited again on July 26. Mrs. Miller and John Ravenscroft called in the evening on July 31; the Millers visited again on Aug. 7, had dinner, and played bowls; and on Aug. 11 Mrs. Miller again visited (Byrd, *Diary, 1739 – 1741*, 143 – 44, 164, 168, 173, 176, 178, 179).

Hugh Miller appears in the letter book of Francis Jerdone, March 4, 1741/42 (Middleton, 380, n.61), and served as an administrator of the estate of Dr. Ebenezer Campbell of Blandford in 1752 (VG14Aug52; rpt. 13W(1)6). A manuscript list of the justices of peace of Prince George Co. for Jan. 18, 1744/45, shows Miller fourth on the court; his father-in-law, Robert Bolling, was chief justice, and his brother-in-law Dr. William Starke (c.1708–c.1755) was second (Va. Hist. Soc. MS). Though RB called him "a professed free-Thinker," Miller (along with JAMES MURRAY) was elected to the vestry of Bristol Parish on Aug. 25, 1746. He attended vestry meetings until Nov. 15, 1757 (Chamberlayne, 122–75). After Miller left Virginia in 1760, ROGER ATKINSON was elected to the vestry in his place.

Miller organized the Blandford Lodge of Freemasons (Nov. 16, 1755; chartered by the Grand Lodge of Scotland on Sept. 9, 1757) and served as its first master (W. M. Brown, 9, 11, 13, 16, 420, 439). When he went to New York in the late summer of 1757, he carried letters to William Byrd III and returned in the fall bringing back letters from Byrd (Tinling, 625, 631). RB said that Miller often during his wife's life "expressed a desire to return to Scotland," and newspaper advertisements bear this out. As early as 1751 he intended to return to Great Britain (VG 16Aug51:32), but his resolve was evidently put off from year to year by his wife's reluctance to leave Virginia (VG 29May52:31, 28Aug52:31; 27Oct52:22). Preparing to depart, he sold two lots (nos. 8 and 9) in Blandford to JOHN BAIRD on Dec. 11, 1759, for £200 (Weisiger, 74). After returning to Glasgow late in 1760, he went to London where he died on Feb. 13, 1762 (*London Magazine*, Feb. 1762, p. 109).

Four children are mentioned in his will, dated Dec. 1, 1761 (proved and filed at Somerset House, London, in March 1762), a young son Hugh Miller and three daughters: first, Anne ("Nancy"), who married Sir PEYTON SKIPWITH; second, Lillias, who married (1) Dr. John Ravenscroft (their son Bishop John Starke Ravenscroft is in the *DAB*) and (2) Patrick Stewart of Borness and Cairnsmore in Galloway, Scotland; and third, Jean (1748–1826), who married her former brother-in-law Sir Peyton Skipwith in 1788. In addition, a son Robert was born and baptized on March 28, 1746; perhaps he died young (Chamberlayne, 342).

MILLER, JANE BOLLING (1722–1756 or 1757), whom RB identified as "a Relation," was his half first cousin once removed. The wife of HUGH MILLER and mother of RB's sweetheart ANNE ("Nancy") MILLER she was the daughter of Robert Bolling (1682–1749), a burgess for Prince George Co., and Anne Meriwether Bolling. (Although many authorities give her mother's maiden name as Cocke, RB recorded "her maiden name was Meriwether" [5W(1)276].) She was the granddaughter of Col. Robert Bolling (1646–1709), the emigrant, of Kippax, Prince George Co., by his second wife, Anne Stith Bolling. Jane was thus a "white" or "Stith" Bolling, as opposed to the "red" or "Indian" Bollings descended from Col. Robert Bolling's first wife, Jane Rolfe Bolling, the granddaughter of Pocahontas and John Rolfe. Jane married Hugh Miller about 1740. For a series of her visits to William Byrd of Westover in 1741, see HUGH MILLER. Three of her siblings are mentioned in RB's "Account": MARY BOLLING STARKE; SUSANNA BOLLING BOLLING; and ROBERT BOLLING (1730–1775). In the beginning of "A Circumstantial Account," RB mentioned that she died in 1756, but in his *Memoir*, 10, he said 1757.

For the children, see the account in HUGH MILLER.

MILNER, JAMES (d. 1772), who, with RB and Dr. JOHN DALGLEISH, appraised the estate of John Herbert of Chesterfield Co. on July 15, 1760 (18V189), was a lawyer of Prince George Co. In 1766, writing under the pseudonym "Dikephilos," he joined RB in publicizing the irregularities of the bailment of Col. John Chiswell in the Virginia newspapers (Lemay, "Bailment," 123 n.20, 134). About 1770 he moved to Halifax, N.C., where he was elected a representative to the N.C. House of Delegates in 1772, only to die that December after a fall from his horse (Grimes, *Abstracts*, 248–49). His very large library is listed in his inventory (Grimes, *Wills and Inventories*, 514–22). An example of his engraved armorial bookplate may be found in the Huntington Library copy of Robert Smith, *A Compleat System of Optics* (Cambridge, 1738), acc. no. 125585.

MITCHELS, where RB and ANNE MILLER had their "very tender Tete a tete" on Aug. 28, 1760, was the primary estate of Col. ALEXANDER and SUSANNA BOLLING. RB located it on the south side of the Appomattox, Prince George Co., about two miles below BROADWAY (*see* RB's map). Robert Bolling, eldest son of Col. Alexander and Susanna Bolling, sold it to THE-ODORICK BLAND, Jr., in 1787. It was a large two-story brick house with a high basement. The main hall, which opened on each end to porches, had a broad winding stairway. The dining room was in the basement; the parlor, library, and ladies' chamber were on the first floor, and bedrooms were on the second floor. "It was of true Virginia Colonial design, with large handsome rooms all fitted out with wainscoting, and panelled work, balusters and handrails." Mitchels burned in 1928 (R. B. Gill, who visited the house in 1925, in WPA report on Susanna Bolling, Va. State Library and Archives).

MORRISON, ALEXANDER (fl. 1759–71), a planter with whom RB spent Monday night, Sept. 15, 1760, lived at Ward's Creek, which flows into the James River just south of Hood's, Prince George Co. He married Anne Bland (1735–82), daughter of Col. Richard Bland (1710–1776), the statesman, and Anne Poythress Bland (Joseph Hunter, 425). He appraised the estate of Henry Harrison in early July 1759 (Weisiger, 70). He was a justice of the peace of Prince George Co., ranking eighth in the lists of Nov. 22, 1764, and Nov.

6, 1766; fourth, June 17 and Oct. 26, 1769; and fifth, April 17, 1771 (McIlwaine, 62, 71, 92, 106). His wife's inventory was taken on Feb. 19, 1782 (Weisiger, 166).

MURRAY, JAMES (c. 1714–1764), at whose home on Sept. 13 WILLIAM BLACK told RB that HUGH MILLER had ordered his children to FLOWER-DE-HUNDRED to sail for Scotland, was a planter, of Prince George Co. and of Athol Braes, Amelia Co. He married Anne Bolling (1718–1800), daughter of Col. John Bolling (1676–1729) of Cobbs and Mary Kennon Bolling (22V107). Anne Bolling Murray was RB's aunt and "of the large stature, high courage, and awe-inspiring bearing of her great progenitor, Powhatan" (Robertson, 59). She lived until Feb. 11, 1800 (*Richmond Argus*, Feb. 18, 1800, p. 3).

On RB's map, "J Murray" is located on the south side of the Appomattox, perhaps a mile from the river, just opposite the point where Swift Creek empties into the Appomattox. Along with ALEXANDER BOLLING, James Murray was appointed a justice of the peace of Prince George Co. on March 4, 1745/46. He was twelfth (and last) on the list of April 20, 1752. And on June 8, 1757, he and Alexander Bolling were both "added to the Quorum" for the Prince George Co. commission (*Exec. Journals*, 5:199, 394, 6:51). He and HUGH MILLER were elected vestrymen of Bristol Parish on June 8, 1757. He served as churchwarden for a year beginning on Nov. 10, 1748, and was reappointed for an additional year beginning on Nov. 6, 1749. He attended his last vestry meeting on July 26, 1763. On Dec. 1, 1764, John Banister was appointed a vestryman "in the room of James Murray Deceased" (Chamberlayne, 122, 132, 135, 185, 190, 432–43).

Evidently the James Murray whose widow married RB's friend JERMAN BAKER in 1773 (PD*VG* 7Je73:31) was the son of this James Murray. James Murray, Jr., was born July 10, 1743, and died about 1770. He appears regularly in the Prince George Co. list of justices from his appointment on Nov. 22, 1764, through Oct. 26, 1769; but on April 17, 1771, the Council directed that "James Murray, who is dead," should be omitted. (McIlwaine, 62, 92, 95; *Exec. Journals*, 6:402, 681.) His younger brother William Murray (1752–1815) inherited Athol Braes, Amelia Co., where in 1796 he often entertained Benjamin Henry Latrobe. At William Murray's, Latrobe compiled a genealogy of the Bolling family and reported that the deceased RB of Chellow had the reputation of "a man of great wit and learning" (Latrobe, 1:122).

NASH, ABNER (1740–1786), whom RB mentioned because MARY HERBERT ("Roxana") CLAIBORNE had some "Engagements" for him in 1760, was a lawyer who served as a burgess from Prince George Co. in 1761–62 (Leonard, 93). He appears thirteenth on the list of justices of the peace of Prince George Co. for Nov. 6, 1766 (when his father John Nash was chief justice, and his older brother, John Nash, Jr., was fourth on the list [McIlwaine, 74]). He moved to North Carolina in 1762 and married (1) Justina Dobbs, the widow of Gov. Arthur Dobbs, and (2) Mary Whiting Jones. In North Carolina he was successively elected delegate, Speaker of the House, governor, 1780–81, and U.S. congressman, 1782–85 (*DAB*).

PETERSON, JOHN (1720/21–1773), at whose home on Sept. 13, 1760, ANNE MILLER told RB she would be glad to leave Virginia (and him!), was a planter of Prince George Co. He was the son of John Peterson of Isle of Wight Co. and married Martha Thweat (b. 1731), daughter of James and Anne Thweat of Palestine, Prince George Co., near Petersburg (Torrence, 2–5). He was an executor of the will of John Thweat, his wife's grandfather, in 1759 (Weisiger, 69).

PRESTWOULD, Middlesex Co., where in 1764 ANNE MILLER received RB's congratulations on her marriage and return to Virginia, was built by Sir Grey Skipwith (d. 1680) and is not to be confused with Prestwould, Mecklenburg Co., which Sir PEYTON SKIPWITH built in 1794 (Turner).

PRINCE GEORGE COUNTY, created out of Charles City Co. in 1702, is on the south side of the Appomattox River, adjoining Dinwiddie Co., and across the river from Chesterfield and Charles City counties (*see* RB's map).

PRINCE GEORGE COURTHOUSE, where BOLLING STARKE, on Sept. 9, 1760, convinced RB not to journey down to see HUGH MILLER, was located about four miles south of the Appomattox River, just above its juncture with the James River (*see* RB's map).

RANDOLPH, MARY ANNE (fl. 1760), of Curles, Henrico Co., referred to in poem no. 1, is unidentified (she is not listed in Cowden).

ROY, JANE WILEY (c. 1745–post 1797), the second wife of HARRY BEVERLEY (c. 1730–1773) (whom RB made the speaker of his revised version of "The Dupe" [poem no. 6]), was the daughter of Richard Roy (c. 1717–c. 1795) and Jane Wiley Roy of Caroline Co. She was a first cousin, not a sister (contrary to RB), of LUCY ROY, both being granddaughters of John and Dorothy Buckner Roy. Beverley married Lucy Roy first; after her death he married Jane in 1765 (Warner, 201–3; Warren, 186–87). In 1797 Jane married, second, Dr. Collin Reddock (Riddick) of Hanover Co. (18VIII).

ROY, LUCY (c. 1743–c. 1763), the first wife of HARRY BEVERLEY (c. 1730–1773) (whom RB makes the speaker of his revised version of "The Dupe" [poem no. 6]), was the daughter of Thomas Roy (1712–1772) and Judith Beverley Kenner Roy (1710–1756), daughter of Capt. Harry Beverley and widow of Rev. Rodham Kenner (d. 1730). Because she and her husband were both grandchildren of Capt. Harry Beverley (d. 1730), the two were first cousins. She was also a first cousin, not a sister (as RB thought), of JANE WILEY ROY, both being granddaughters of John and Dorothy Buckner Roy (Warner, 201–3). She died shortly after her marriage (Warren, 187).

SAPPONY. Evidently the upper branches of the Nottoway River, crossed by the Sappony Road (see 15V239), were loosely called Sappony. RB and his friends started out "to visit some Friends on Sappony River" on Jan. 13 and returned "from Sappony" on Jan. 18. On the trip he called upon BOLLING STARKE, ROBERT WALKER, and HERBERT HAYNES. Sappony Creek flows into the Nottoway River about twenty-five miles south of Petersburg (Fry and Jefferson map).

SCOTT, ISABEL (fl. 1762), referred to in RB's "Letter to Jerman Baker, 1762" (poem no. 14), may be the Isabel Scott who was a daughter of James Scott of Amelia Co. He mentioned her in his will, dated Dec. 24, 1759, and proved March 26, 1761 (*Va. Geneal.* 18:119).

SKIPWITH, Sir PEYTON (1740–1805), planter, whose attachment to ANNE MILLER was questioned by RB on Jan. 31, 1760, when she and RB spent the night at COBBS, was the son of Sir William and Elizabeth Smith Skipwith, of Prestwould, Middlesex Co. (*Burke's Peerage*, 2459). He voyaged to Scotland in Nov. 1762 to court her. RB addressed poem no. 15, "The Exile," to Skipwith. Skipwith and Anne Miller returned to Virginia in 1764 and married there. Sir Peyton loaned RB £1.3.9 at "Albemarle old Court House" in 1764 (Skipwith Papers, box 22, Ledger 1762–65, p. 4, College of William and Mary). On April 25, 1765, he was in Williamsburg, gambling with William Byrd III at Mrs. Vobe's tavern (Anon., "Journal," 742). The couple settled at Greencrofts (which Anne Miller inherited), on the Appomattox, Prince George Co., and then moved in 1769 to Elm Hill, Mecklenburg Co. (another of her inheritances).

　　Skipwith was appointed a justice of the peace for Prince George Co. on Nov. 22, 1764, twelfth on the list; he was twelfth again on the list of Nov. 6, 1766, and eighth on that of June 17, 1769 (*Exec. Journals*, 6:681; McIlwaine, 62, 71, 92). After the move to Elm Hill, he appears tenth on the Mecklenburg Co. list of Oct. 23, 1769, thereby causing Samuel Hopkins, twelfth on that list, to refuse to serve "on account of Sir Peyton Skipwith's being put higher in the list than himself" (*Exec. Journals*, 6:141; McIlwaine, 95). The clerk (carelessly?) reported Skipwith as eight on the Prince George list on Oct. 26, 1769 (McIlwaine, 95); but on April 17, 1771, the Council noted that he should be omitted from the Prince George Co. commission because he had "removed to another County." He was again tenth on the Mecklenburg Co. list of May 8, 1771 (*Exec. Journals*, 6:329, 402; McIlwaine, 109).

He and Anne Miller had four children before her death in 1779 (*see* Introduction). He was elected to the Mecklenburg Co. Committee of Correspondence on May 8, 1775 (*Rev. Va.*, 3:105), but he was at best a lukewarm patriot. In 1778 the couple moved to Hog Island, Surry Co. He was tried on June 4, 1781, for treason and found innocent (Kesler, 74). Sabine (2:309) lists him as a loyalist, but Skipwith evidently took no active part in the war, remained in the country, and does not appear in Palmer's revision of Sabine. In the 1780s, again living in Mecklenburg Co., he was among the one hundred richest men in Virginia (Main, 382–83).

In 1788 he married Jean Miller (1748–1826), Anne Miller's younger sister. Jefferson included the news in a list of marriages and deaths sent to William Short. Short replied: "I cannot find out who the Miss Miller is whom Sir P. Skipwith has married unless it be his wife's sister. This will be an uncommon though not an unexampled thing in America" (Jefferson, 14:530, 608). (For the children of Jean and Peyton, see Abraham.) Skipwith built Prestwould, Mecklenburg Co., in 1794.

In 1796 Benjamin Henry Latrobe noted that "Sir Peyton Skipwith is one of the very few who keep up their title in this country. The title of Baronet is a phantom even *in England*, having no real priviledge annexed to it, here it is the lank Ghost of a phantom, the shadow of a shade" (Latrobe, 1:144). Alas, there seems to be no truth in the legend that he won his Mecklenburg Co. lands in a card game with William Byrd III (Elliott). Sir Peyton died on Oct. 8, 1805 (*Richmond Argus*, Oct. 19, 1805; *Va. Gaz. & Genl. Advertiser*, Oct. 26, 1805, p. 3).

STARKE, BOLLING (1733–1788), whom RB, ANNE MILLER, and a group of friends visited on the way to the Sappony River on Jan. 13, 1760, and who, on Sept. 4, 1760, wrote RB of JAMES JOHNSON's opposition to the courtship, was RB's half second cousin and Anne Miller's first cousin. The son of Dr. William Starke and MARY ANN BOLLING STARKE, and the elder brother of WILLIAM STARKE, Jr., and ELIZABETH STARKE, he was born Sept. 21, 1733, and baptized the following Nov. 11 (Chamberlayne, 366). He was a planter, merchant, and attorney. On Nov. 4, 1754, he witnessed the will of John Lewis (Weisiger, 175); on Dec. 11, 1759, he witnessed the deed of HUGH MILLER's sale of two lots in Blandford to JOHN BAIRD (ibid., 74). His mother gave him three slaves on May 11, 1760 (ibid., 79). He served as a justice of the peace for Dinwiddie Co., ranking fifth in the lists of Aug. 1, 1763 (when he was sheriff of the county), and Nov. 24, 1766; third on Nov. 17, 1769,

July 17 and Nov. 6, 1771; and second on Feb. 12, 1774 (McIlwaine, 68, 75, 95, 111, 112, 124). Lewis Burwell recorded that Starke shipped 100 hogsheads of tobacco in 1773 and 123 in 1774 (Thomson, 406). He served as burgess from Dinwiddie Co. in the assemblies of 1769 and 1769–71; as a member of the Fifth Virginia Convention, May 5–July 5, 1776 (*Rev. Va.*, 6:391, 392 n.2); as a member of the House of Delegates in 1776, 1777–78; as a member of the Council in 1781; and as Virginia state auditor in 1781 and 1786 (Leonard, 97, 99, 119, 122, 125). He died in Richmond on Jan. 25, 1788 (*Va. Independent Chronicle*, Jan. 30, 1788).

STARKE (later Walker), ELIZABETH ("Betsy") (1744–1828), who made CARTER HENRY HARRISON miserable on Jan. 31, 1760, by flirting with RB, was the youngest daughter of Dr. William Starke and MARY ANN BOLLING STARKE and the younger sister of BOLLING STARKE and WILLIAM STARKE, Jr. RB addressed "The Dream" (poem no. 2) to her in April 1760, after spending the night in her short bed while she was away. In a poem (no. 10) addressed to her brother William in Oct. 1760, RB revealed that her childhood nickname "Starkey" was still used, though she had (by age seventeen) become a "Tempestiva Viro."

She married ROBERT WALKER about 1762, lived at Kingston Plantation, Dinwiddie Co., and had twenty children, eleven of whom lived to adulthood (see Nicholson). She died on June 23, 1828, age eighty-four (ibid., 26).

STARKE, MARY ANN BOLLING (1717/18–post 1769), who first gave RB a hint that ANNE MILLER cared for him, was Anne Miller's aunt and RB's half first cousin once removed. In 1727 she married Dr. William Starke (c. 1708–c.1755), who evidently lived in York Co. until about 1730, when he moved to BROADWAY, Prince George Co. She was the daughter of Robert Bolling (1682–1749) of Prince George Co. and Anne Meriwether Bolling, and the elder sister of SUSANNA BOLLING BOLLING, JANE BOLLING MILLER, and ROBERT BOLLING (1730–1775). Her husband William Starke was third on the commission for the justices of the peace on Oct. 2, 1774, for Prince George Co.; second on the manuscript list for Jan. 18, 1744/45 (Va. Hist. Soc. MS); and chief justice in the list of April 30, 1752 (*Exec. Journals*, 5:162, 394). Rind's *Va. Gaz.* of July 27, 1769, p. 23, reported that she was one of five notable "widow ladies" who signed the Nonimportation Association of May 17, 1769.

She had six children. First, Rebecca, who married (1) Dr. John Ravenscroft, who visited William Byrd at Westover in the company of HUGH MILLER on March 16, 1741, and who took his M.D. at Edinburgh in 1770 (*List*,

10) (their son Dr. John Ravenscroft married his cousin Lillias Miller, grand-daughter of JANE and HUGH MILLER), and (2) George McMurdo. Second, BOLLING STARKE. Third, Robert. Fourth, Dr. WILLIAM STARKE, Jr. Fifth, Richard Starke (d. 1772), whose *The Office and Authority of a Justice of the Peace* (Williamsburg: Purdie and Dixon, 1774) appeared posthumously. And sixth, ELIZABETH STARKE.

STARKE, Dr. WILLIAM, Jr. (c.1736–post 1779), of Petersburg, Prince George Co., to whom RB addressed poem no. 10 when returning the razors he had borrowed, was the son of MARY ANN BOLLING STARKE and the brother of BOLLING STARKE and ELIZABETH STARKE. He served as a lieutenant in the Virginia Regiment in 1755 and 1756, when he raised George Washington's ire by supporting the claims to seniority of Capt. John Dagworthy. For this, he was subjected to a court of inquiry at Fort Cumberland on Jan. 16, 1756. By March, he declared that he would resign rather than serve under Capt. Peter Hog. He was lured into the Indian ambush where Capt. John Fenton Mercer and others were killed outside Edwards's fort on April 18. He served on the court-martial that exonerated Lt. John Edward Lomax as well as the court-martial that condemned Sgt. Nathan Lewis to death for cowardice on the occasion. In July, commanded to serve under Captain Hog, he made good his threat and resigned (Washington, *Papers*, 2:289n.3, 327, 3:17–18, 72–74, 77–79, 250, 272n.8, 314, 319n.15).

His father left him the estate BROADWAY, Prince George Co., which he sold in 1766 (Hening, 8:289–91; Fauquier, 1533–34). He was a justice of the peace of Prince George Co., ranking ninth on the lists of Nov. 22, 1764, and Nov. 6, 1766; fifth on the lists of June 17 and Oct. 26, 1769 (when he was sheriff of the county); and sixth on April 17, 1771. Evidently he moved to Brunswick Co., for he was added to the commission of the peace there on June 17, 1774, and ranked twelfth (McIlwaine, 62, 71, 92, 95, 106, 127). He owned a drugstore in Petersburg and advertised for an apothecary to run it in May 1768 (PD*VG* 5May68:22). He and Dr. THEODORICK BLAND, Jr., practiced medicine in partnership in Petersburg until 1771, when he advertised (PD*VG* 28Mar71:31) his own medical practice. He married Mary Bassett Daingerfield in Nov. 1779 (D*VG* 6N79:31). Blanton (352) believes that he is probably the same Dr. William Starke who served as a surgeon in the Revolution.

TAGGART, Mr. (Cleland?) (fl. 1762), with whom PEYTON SKIPWITH took passage for Scotland in 1762 (though he sailed with another ship) may be Capt. Cleland Taggart, of the *Speedwell*, who was sailing in the 1750s (*VG* 20Oct52:21 and 28Mar55:22).

WALKER, ROBERT (1729–1797), "who had prepared an Entertainment" for RB, ANNE MILLER, ELIZABETH STARKE, CARTER HENRY HARRISON, and other friends on Jan. 14, 1760, lived at Kingston Plantation, on the Sappony River, Dinwiddie Co. He was the son of David and Mary Munford Walker. A planter, he later married ELIZABETH STARKE, the sister of BOLLING STARKE and daughter of MARY ANN BOLLING STARKE. A justice of the peace from Dinwiddie Co., he ranked seventh on the list of Aug. 1, 1763; eighth, Aug. 16, 1765, and Nov. 24, 1766; fifth, Nov. 17, 1769, July 17 and Nov. 6, 1771; and fourth, Feb. 12, 1774 (McIlwaine, 68 (2), 75, 95, 111, 112, 124). His letter to THEODORICK BLAND, Jr., dated July 25, 1764, survives in the Ruffin Papers, University of Virginia Library. After the Revolution, Walker was the chief justice of the Dinwiddie Court "for many years" (14T26; Nicholson, 26). By 1782 his personal property included fifty-two slaves (26W(1)258). He was an executor of the will of Bolling Starke in 1788. During the 1790s he built Kingston House, Dinwiddie Co. For his children, see ELIZABETH STARKE.

Bibliography

Abraham, Mildred K. "The Library of Lady Jean Skipwith." *Virginia Magazine of History and Biography* 91 (1983): 296–347.

Alumni Cantabrigiensis . . . to 1900. Comp. John Venn and John A. Venn. 10 vols. Cambridge: University Press, 1922–54.

Anderson, Sterling P. *Prestwould and Its Builders.* Clarksville, Va.: APVA, Roanoke River Branch, Boydton Museum, 1963.

Anonymous. *Funny Stories, or, The American Jester.* Worcester, Mass.: I. Thomas, 1795. Evans no. 28720.

——. "Journal of a French Traveller in the Colonies, 1765." *American Historical Review* 26 (1921): 726–47; 27 (1922): 70–89.

Ariès, Philippe. *Centuries of Childhood: A Social History of Family Life.* Tr. Robert Baldick. New York: Knopf, 1962.

Ariosto, Ludovico. *Opera.* Ed. Mario Apollonio. Milan: Rizzoli, 1944.

——. *Opera minori.* Ed. Cesare Segre. Milano: Riccardo Ricciardi, 1954.

——. *Orlando Furioso.* Tr. John Harrington (1591), ed. Robert McNulty. London: Oxford University Press, 1972.

——. *Orlando Furioso.* Tr. William Stewart Rose, ed. Stewart A. Baker and A. Bartlett Giamatti. Indianapolis: Bobbs-Merrill, 1968.

Bailyn, Bernard. "Politics and Social Structure in Virginia." *Seventeenth-Century America: Essays in Colonial History.* Ed. James Morton Smith. Chapel Hill: University of North Carolina Press, 1959. Pp. 90–115.

Bedwell, C. E. A. "American Middle Templars." *American Historical Review* 25 (1920): 680–89.

Beverley, William. "Diary of William Beverley of 'Blandfield' during a Visit to England, 1750." [Ed. William G. Stanard.] *Virginia Magazine of History and Biography* 36 (1928): 27–35, 161–69.

Biographical Directory of the American Congress, 1774–1971. Washington, D.C.: U.S. Government Printing Office, 1971.

Black, William. "Journal of William Black, 1744." Ed. R. Alonzo Brock. *Pennsylvania Magazine of History and Biography* 1 (1877): 117–32, 233–49, 404–19; 2 (1878): 40–49.

Black's Law Dictionary. 5th ed. St. Paul: West Publishing Co., 1979.

Bland family chart. "Genealogical chart of the Bland family drawn c. 1825 for John Randolph of Roanoke from a copy compiled c. 1760." Manuscript, Virginia Historical Society, Richmond.

Blanton, Wyndham B. *Medicine in Virginia in the Eighteenth Century*. Richmond: Garrett & Massie, 1931.

Boatner, Mark M., III. *Encyclopedia of the American Revolution*. Bicentennial Edition. New York: David McKay Co., 1976.

Boccaccio, Giovanni. *Decameron*. Tr. Mark Musa and Peter Bondanella. New York: Norton, 1982.

Bolling, Robert. "A Collection of Diverting Anecdotes, Bon-Mots, and Other Trifling Pieces, 1764." Manuscript volume. Huntington Library, San Marino, Calif. Acc. no. BR 163.

———. "La Gazzetta di Parnaso; or Poems, Imitations, Translations, &c." Manuscript volume of Bolling's poetry. Huntington Library, San Marino, Calif. Acc. no. BR 73.

———. "Hilarodiana." Manuscript volume of Bolling's poetry. Private collection. Microfilm at the University of Virginia Library.

———. *A Memoir of a Portion of the Bolling Family*. Tr. John Robertson, Jr., ed. T[homas] H. W[ynne]. Richmond: W. H. Wade & Co., 1868.

———. "A Pathetic Soliloquy." Manuscript Division, Miscellaneous personal papers collection, Library of Congress. (Nineteenth-century copy of Bolling's prose lament on the death of his wife Mary Burton Bolling. One folded sheet of nineteenth-century paper.)

———. "Pieces concerning Vineyards & Their Establishment in Virginia." Manuscript volume, dated "Chellow, Buckingham co., 1773." Huntington Library, San Marino, Calif. Acc. no. BR 64.

Boucher, Jonathan. *Reminiscences of an American Loyalist*. Boston: Houghton Mifflin, 1925.

Brandow, James C. "A Visit to Virginia in 1755." *Virginia Genealogist* 29 (1985): 29–31.

Bridenbaugh, Carl. "Violence and Virtue in Virginia, 1766: or, The Importance of the Trivial." *Proceedings of the Massachusetts Historical Society* 76 (1964): 1–29.

Brown, Stuart E., Jr., Lorraine F. Myers, and Eileen M. Chappel. *Pocahontas' Descendants*. Berryville, Va.: The Pocahontas Foundation, 1985.

Brown, William Mosely, ed. *Blandford Lodge No. 3, A.F. & A.M. Petersburg, Va: A Bicentennial History*. Petersburg, Va.: Plummer Printing Co., 1957.

Buchanan, George. *The Jephtha and Baptist*. Tr. Alexander Gibb. Edinburgh: J. Moodie Miller, 1870.

——. *Jephthanes, sive votum tragaedia*. In *Georgii Buchanani Scoti poemata quae extant*. Amsterlaedami: Apud Henricum Wetstenium, 1687.

Burke, John. *Burke's Peerage and Baronetage*. Ed. Peter Townend. London: Burke's Peerage, 1970.

——. *A Genealogical and Heraldic Dictionary of the Landed Gentry*. Ed. Peter Townend. 3 vols. London: Burke's Peerage, 1964–72.

Burnaby, Andrew. *Burnaby's Travels through North America*. Ed. Rufus Rockwell Wilson. New York: A. Wessels Co., 1904.

Burney, Charles. *Memoirs of the Life and Writings of the Abate Metastasio*. 2 vols. London: G. G. and J. Robinson, 1796.

Burwell, George H. *Record of the Burwell Family*. 1908; rpt. in Stuart E. Brown and Ann B. Brown, *Carter Hall*. Berryville, Va.: Virginia Book Co., 1978.

Byrd, William, II. *Another Secret Diary of William Byrd of Westover, 1739–1741, with Letters and Literary Exercises, 1696–1726*. Ed. Maude H. Woodfin, tr. Marion Tinling. Richmond: Dietz Press, 1942.

——. *The London Diary (1717–1721) and Other Writings*. Ed. Louis B. Wright and Marion Tinling. New York: Oxford University Press, 1958.

——. *The Prose Works of William Byrd of Westover*. Ed. Louis B. Wright. Cambridge: Harvard University Press, 1966.

——. *The Secret Diary of William Byrd of Westover, 1709–1712*. Ed. Louis B. Wright and Marion Tinling. Richmond: Dietz Press, 1941.

Calhoon, Robert M. "'A Sorrowful Spectator of These Tumultuous Times': Robert Beverley Describes the Coming of the Revolution." *Virginia Magazine of History and Biography* 73 (1965): 41–55.

———. "'Unhinging Former Intimacies': Robert Beverley's Perception of the Pre-Revolutionary Controversy, 1761–1775." *South Atlantic Quarterly* 68 (1969): 246–61.

Campbell, Charles, ed. *The Bland Papers*. 2 vols. Petersburg, Va.: E. and J. C. Ruffin, 1840–43.

Cappon, Lester J., and Stella F. Duff, comps. *Virginia Gazette Index, 1736–1780*. 2 vols. Williamsburg, Va.: Institute of Early American History and Culture, 1950.

Carr, Lois Green. "The Foundations of Social Order: Local Government in Colonial Maryland." In *Town and Country: Essays on the Structure of Local Government in the American Colonies*. Ed. Bruce C. Daniels. Middletown, Conn.: Wesleyan University Press, 1978. Pp. 77–110.

Carson, Jane. *Colonial Virginians at Play*. Williamsburg, Va.: Colonial Williamsburg Foundation, 1965.

———. *Travelers in Tidewater Virginia, 1700–1800: A Bibliography*. Charlottesville: University Press of Virginia, 1965.

Carter, Landon. *The Diary of Landon Carter of Sabine Hall 1752–1788*. Ed. Jack P. Greene. 2 vols. Charlottesville: University Press of Virginia, 1965.

"Carter Tree." Manuscript, Virginia Historical Society.

Chamberlayne, Churchill Gibson, ed. *The Vestry Book and Register of Bristol Parish, Virginia, 1720–1789*. Richmond: C. G. Chamberlayne, 1898.

Chastellux, François Jean, marquis de. *Travels in North-America, in the Years 1780, 1781, and 1782*. 2 vols. Tr. from the French by an English Gentleman . . . with Notes. London: G. G. J. & J. Robinson, 1787.

Chiabrera, Gabriello. *Canzonetti rime varie dialoghi*, ed. Luigi Negri. Torinese: Unione Tipografico, Deitrice, 1968.

Cocke, Lonnie Doss, and Virginia Webb Cocke. *Cockes and Cousins*. Vol. 1: *Descendants of Richard Cocke (ca. 1600–1665)*. Vol. 2: *Descendants of Thomas Cocke (ca. 1639–1697)*. Winston-Salem, N.C.: n.p., 1967–74.

Coles, William B. *The Coles Family of Virginia*. New York: 1931.

Cowden, Gerald Steffens. "The Randolphs of Turkey Island: A Prosopography of the First Three Generations, 1650–1806." Ph.D. diss.: College of William and Mary, 1977.

Cresswell, Nicholas. *The Journal of Nicholas Cresswell, 1774–1777.* New York: Dial Press, 1924.

Cutten, George Barton. *The Silversmiths of Virginia . . . to 1850.* Richmond: Dietz Press, 1952.

Dante. *The Divine Comedy of Dante Alighieri: Inferno.* Tr. Allen Mandelbaum. Berkeley: University of California Press, 1980.

Davis, Richard Beale. *Intellectual Life in the Colonial South, 1585–1763.* 3 vols. Knoxville: University of Tennessee Press, 1978.

DeLancey, Heywood Marshall. *Lives of the Bishops of North Carolina.* Raleigh, N.C.: A. Williams & Co., 1910.

Dewey, Frank L. "The Norfolk Anti-Inoculation Riots." *Virginia Magazine of History and Biography* 91 (1983): 39–53.

———. *Thomas Jefferson, Lawyer.* Charlottesville: University Press of Virginia, 1986.

Dictionary of North Carolina Biography. Ed. William S. Powell. Chapel Hill: University of North Carolina Press, 1979–.

Dolmetsch, Carl R. "William Byrd II: Comic Dramatist." *Early American Literature* 6, no. 1 (1971): 18–30.

Dorman, John Frederick. "A Guide to the Counties of Virginia: Buckingham County." *Virginia Genealogist* 6 (1962): 121–24.

Dryden, John. *Works.* Ed. Sir Walter Scott, rev. George Saintsbury. 18 vols. Edinburgh: William Paterson, 1882–93.

Dumbauld, Edward. *Thomas Jefferson and the Law.* Norman: University of Oklahoma Press, 1978.

[Du Ponceau, Pierre Etienne] "Observator." "An Account of Two Americans of Extraordinary Genius in Poetry and Music." *Columbian Magazine* 2 (April 1788): 211–13, 230.

———. "The Autobiography of Peter Stephen Du Ponceau." Ed. James L. Whitehead. *Pennsylvania Magazine of History and Biography* 63 (1939): 189–227, 311–43, 432–61.

Elliott, Herbert A. "Sir Peyton Skipwith and the Byrd Land." *Virginia Magazine of History and Biography* 80 (1972): 52–59.

Enys, John. *The American Journals of Lt. John Enys*. Ed. Elizabeth Cometti. Syracuse, N.Y.: Syracuse University Press, 1976.

Evans, Charles. *American Bibliography: A Chronological Bibliography . . . [through 1800]*. 14 vols. Chicago et al.: Evans et al., 1903–59.

Executive Journals of the Council of Colonial Virginia. Eds. H. R. McIlwaine and Benjamin Hillman. 6 vols. Richmond: Virginia State Library, 1925–66.

Fauquier, Francis. *The Official Papers of Francis Fauquier, Lieutenant Governor of Virginia, 1758–1768*. Ed. George Reese. 3 vols. Charlottesville: University Press of Virginia, 1980–83.

Fithian, Philip Vickers. *Journal and Letters of Philip Vickers Fithian, 1773–1774: A Plantation Tutor of the Old Dominion*. Ed. Hunter Dickinson Farish. 1943; rpt. Williamsburg, Va.: Colonial Williamsburg, Inc., 1965.

Franklin, Benjamin. *Benjamin Franklin: Writings*. Ed. J. A. Leo Lemay. New York: Library of America, 1987.

——. *The Papers of Benjamin Franklin*. Ed. Leonard W. Labaree et al. New Haven: Yale University Press, 1959–.

Freeman, Douglas Southall. *George Washington*. 7 vols. New York: Scribner's, 1949–57.

The Fry & Jefferson Map of Virginia and Maryland: Facsimiles of the 1754 and 1794 Printings with an Index. Foreword by Dumas Malone; Index by Mary Catharine Murphy. Charlottesville: University Press of Virginia, 1966.

Gaines, William H., Jr. "Courthouses of Charles City and Prince Georges Counties." *Virginia Cavalcade* 18 (Summer 1968): 5–12.

Greene, G. S., and Louise Brownell Clarke. *The Greenes of Rhode Island*. New York: Knickerbocker Press, 1903.

Griffith, Lucille. "English Education for Virginia Youth: Some Eighteenth-Century Ambler Family Letters." *Virginia Magazine of History and Biography* 69 (1961): 7–27.

Grimes, J[ohn] Byran. *Abstracts of North Carolina Wills*. Raleigh, N.C., 1910; rpt. Baltimore: Genealogical Publishing Co., 1967.

————. *North Carolina Wills and Inventories*. Raleigh, N.C.: Edwards & Broughton, 1912.

Guarini, Battista. *Il Pastor Fido*. Tr. Richard Fanshaw, ed. J. H. Whitfield. Edinburgh Bilingual Library, no. 11. Austin: University of Texas Press, 1976.

Hamilton, Dr. Alexander. *Gentleman's Progress: The Itinerarium of Dr. Alexander Hamilton*. Ed. Carl Bridenbaugh. Chapel Hill: University of North Carolina Press, 1948.

Harrison, Margaret Tressler Scott. "Sketch of the Family of Carter Henry Harrison (1736–1783). . . ." Hampton, Va., 1959. Mimeographed. Copy at Swem Library, the College of William and Mary.

Harrower, John. *The Journal of John Harrower, an Indentured Servant in the Colony of Virginia, 1773–1776*. Ed. Edward Miles Riley. New York: Holt, Rinehart, & Winston, 1963.

Hazard, Ebenezer. "The Journal of Ebenezer Hazard in Virginia, 1777." Ed. Fred Shelley. *Virginia Magazine of History and Biography* 62 (1954): 400–23.

Hemphill, John M., II. "John Wayles Rates His Neighbours." *Virginia Magazine of History and Biography* 66 (1958): 302–6.

Henderson, Patrick. "Smallpox and Patriotism: the Norfolk Riots, 1768–1769." *Virginia Magazine of History and Biography* 73 (1965): 413–24.

Hening, William Waller, ed. *The Statutes at Large: Being a Collection of All the Laws of Virginia from the First Session of the Legislature, in the Year 1619*. 13 vols. New York, Philadelphia, and Richmond: various publishers, 1819–23.

Henley, Bernard J., comp. *Marriages and Deaths from Richmond, Virginia, Newspapers, 1780–1820*. Richmond: Virginia Genealogical Society, 1983.

Hesiod. *Theogony*. In *The Homeric Hymns: Fragments of the Epic Cycle Homerica*. Tr. Hugh G. Evelyn-White. 2d ed. Loeb Classical Library. Cambridge: Harvard University Press, 1936. Pp. 79–153.

Hiden, Martha W. *How Justice Grew: Virginia Counties: An Abstract of Their Formation*. Williamsburg, Va.: 350th Anniversary Celebration Corporation, 1957.

Horace. *The Odes and Epodes*. Tr. C. E. Bennett. 1914; rpt. Loeb Classical Library, Cambridge: Harvard University Press, 1964.

——. *Satires, Epistles, and Ars Poetica.* Tr. H. R. Fairclough. 1926; rpt. Loeb Classical Library, Cambridge: Harvard University Press, 1966.

Hunter, Joseph. *Familial Minorum Gentium.* Ed. John W. Clay. Vol. 2. London: Harleian Society (vol. 40), 1895.

Hunter, Robert, Jr. *Quebec to Carolina in 1785–1786.* Ed. Louis B. Wright and Marion Tinling. San Marino, Calif.: Huntington Library, 1943.

Isaac, Rhys. *The Transformation of Virginia, 1740–1790.* Chapel Hill: University of North Carolina Press, 1982.

Jefferson, Thomas. *Papers.* Ed. Julian Boyd et al. Princeton, N.J.: Princeton University Press, 1951–.

Jones, E[dward] Alfred. *American Members of the Inns of Court.* London: St. Catherine Press, 1924.

Journals of the House of Burgesses of Virginia, 1761–1765. Ed. John Pendleton Kennedy. Richmond: Virginia State Library, 1907.

Kagle, Steven E. *American Diary Literature, 1620–1799.* Boston: Twayne, 1979.

Kesler, Benjamin Robert. "The Skipwith Family in Colonial Virginia." M.A. thesis, University of Virginia, 1938.

King, George H. S. "Will of Colonel John Chiswell (c. 1710–1766)." *Virginia Genealogical Quarterly Bulletin* 7 (1967): 77–83.

Knight, Sarah Kemble. *The Journal of Madam Knight.* Ed. George Parker Winship. 1920; rpt. New York: Peter Smith, 1935.

Kukla, Jon. "Order and Chaos in Early America: Political and Social Stability in Pre-Restoration Virginia." *American Historical Review* 90 (1985): 275–98.

Kulikoff, Allan. *Tobacco and Slaves: The Development of Southern Culture in the Chesapeake, 1680–1800.* Chapel Hill: University of North Carolina Press, 1986.

Latrobe, Benjamin Henry. *The Virginia Journals of Benjamin Henry Latrobe.* Ed. Edward C. Carter II et al. 2 vols. New Haven: Yale University Press, 1977.

Lemay, J. A. Leo. *A Calendar of American Poetry in the Colonial Newspapers and Magazines and in the Major English Magazines through 1765.* Worcester, Mass.: American Antiquarian Society, 1972.

——. Review of Anne Y. Zimmer, *Jonathan Boucher: Loyalist in Exile.* In *Virginia Magazine of History and Biography* 87 (1979): 108–9.

———. "Robert Beverley's *History and Present State of Virginia* and the Emerging American Political Ideology." In *American Letters and the Historical Consciousness: Essays in Honor of Lewis P. Simpson.* Ed. J. Gerald Kennedy and Daniel Mark Fogel. Baton Rouge: Louisiana State University Press, 1987. Pp. 67–111.

———. "Robert Bolling and the Bailment of Colonel Chiswell." *Early American Literature* 6 (1971): 99–142.

———. "Southern Colonial Grotesque: Robert Bolling's 'Neanthe.'" *Mississippi Quarterly* 35 (1982): 97–126.

Leonard, Cynthia Miller. *The General Assembly of Virginia, July 30, 1619–Jan. 11, 1978: A Bicentennial Register of Members.* Richmond: Virginia State Library, 1978.

Lewis, Jan. *The Pursuit of Happiness: Family and Values in Jefferson's Virginia.* Cambridge: Cambridge University Press, 1983.

Lippi, Lorenzo. *Il Malmantile.* 2 vols. Firenze: Nestenus & Moucke, 1731. Bolling's copy at Huntington Library, acc. no. 129416.

List of the Graduates in Medicine in the University of Edinburgh from 1705–1864. Edinburgh: Neill & Co., 1867.

Lockridge, Kenneth A. *The Diary, and Life, of William Byrd II of Virginia, 1674–1744.* Chapel Hill: University of North Carolina Press, 1987.

Lucan. *Pharsalia.* Tr. J. D. Duff. 1928; rpt. Loeb Classical Library, Cambridge: Harvard University Press, 1977.

McGill, John. *The Beverly Family of Virginia.* Columbia, S.C.: R. L. Bryan Co., 1956. (See also the review in *Virginia Magazine of History and Biography* 65 [1957]: 516–17 by John F. Dorman.)

McIlwaine, Herbert R. "Justices of the Peace of Colonial Virginia [1757–1775]." *Bulletin of the Virginia State Library* 14 (1921): 41–149.

McKay, David P., and Richard Crawford. *William Billings of Boston: 18th Century Composer.* Princeton, N.J.: Princeton University Press, 1975.

Main, Jackson T. "The One Hundred." *William and Mary Quarterly,* 3d ser., 11 (1954): 334–84.

Mason, Frances N., ed. *John Norton & Sons Merchants of London and Virginia 1750 to 1795.* Richmond: Dietz Press, 1937.

Mason, George. *Papers*. Ed. Robert A. Rutland. 3 vols. Chapel Hill: University of North Carolina Press, 1970.

Mays, David J. *Sketch of William Fleming, the Third President of the Supreme Court of Appeals of Virginia*. Richmond: 1928.

Meade, William. *Old Churches, Ministers, and Families of Virginia*. 2 vols. Philadelphia: Lippincott, 1857.

Metastasio, Pietro. *Tutte le opere di Pietro Metastasio*. Ed. Bruno Brunelli. 5 vols. Verona: Montadori, 1947.

Micklus, Robert. "The Delightful Instruction of Dr. Alexander Hamilton's *Itinerarium*." *American Literature* 60 (1988): 359–84.

Middleton, Arthur P. *Tobacco Coast*. Newport News, Va.: Mariners' Museum, 1953.

Miller, Jon Charles. "*A Collection of Plays and Poems, by the Late Col. Robert Munford, of Mecklenburg County, in the State of Virginia:* A Critical Edition." Ph.D. diss., University of North Carolina, Chapel Hill, 1979.

Molière. [Jean Baptiste Poquelin.] *L'école des femmes*. Ed. S. Rossat-Mignod. Paris: Editions Sociales, 1964.

——. *The Plays of Molière*. Tr. A. R. Waller. Edinburgh: John Grant, 1907.

Morgan, Edmund S. *Virginians at Home: Family Life in the Eighteenth Century*. Williamsburg, Va.: Colonial Williamsburg Foundation, 1952.

Morrison, A. J., ed. "Letters of Roger Atkinson, 1769–1776." *Virginia Magazine of History and Biography* 15 (1908): 345–59.

Munford, Robert. *A Collection of Plays and Poems, by the Late Col. Robert Munford*. Ed. William Munford. Petersburg, Va.: W. Prentis, 1798. Evans no. 34158.

Nathan, Hans. *William Billings: Data and Documents*. Detroit: Information Coordinators for the College Music Society, 1976.

Nicholson, Lee. "The Walker Family." *Tyler's Historical and Genealogical Quarterly* 14 (1932–33): 25–43.

Norris, Walter B. "Some Recently Found Poems on the Calverts." *Maryland Historical Magazine* 32 (1937): 112–35.

Nottingham, Stratton, comp. *The Marriage License Bonds of Northhampton County,*

Virginia, from 1706 to 1854. 1929; rpt. Baltimore: Genealogical Publishing Co., 1974.

O'Dell, Jeffrey M. *Chesterfield County: Early Architecture and Historic Sites.* Chesterfield Co., Va.: [Chesterfield County Planning Department], 1983.

[Orr, Lucinda Lee.] *Journal of a Young Lady of Virginia.* Baltimore: John Murphy and Co., 1871.

Ovid. *The Art of Love and Other Poems.* Tr. J. H. Zoyley, 2d ed., rev. G. P. Gould. Loeb Classical Library. Cambridge: Harvard University Press, 1979.

——. *Metamorphoses.* Tr. Frank Justus Miller. New York: Putnam, 1925.

——. *Tristia.* Tr. Arthur Leslie Wheeler. Loeb Classical Library. Cambridge: Harvard University Press, 1939.

Palmer, Gregory. *Biographical Sketches of Loyalists of the American Revolution.* Westport, Conn.: Meckler, 1984.

Peacock, Matthew Henry. *History of the Free Grammar School of Queen Elizabeth at Wakefield.* Wakefield: W. H. Milnes, 1892.

Petrarch, Francesco. *Petrarch's Lyric Poems.* Tr. Robert M. Durling. Cambridge: Harvard University Press, 1976.

Quincy, Josiah, Jr. "Journal of Josiah Quincy, Junior, 1773." *Proceedings of the Massachusetts Historical Society* 49 (1915–16): 424–81.

Reeves, Enos. "Extracts from the Letter-Books of Lieutenant Enos Reeves, of the Pennsylvania Line." Ed. John B. Reeves. *Pennsylvania Magazine of History and Biography* 20 (1896–97): 302–14, 456–72; 21 (1897–98): 72–85, 235–56, 372–91, 466–76.

Revolutionary Virginia: The Road to Independence. Ed. William J. Van Schreeven, Robert L. Scribner, and Brent Tarter. 7 vols. Charlottesville: University Press of Virginia, 1973–83.

Rice, Howard C., Jr., and Anne S. K. Brown, eds. *The American Campaigns of Rochambeau's Army, 1780, 1781, 1782, 1783.* 2 vols. Princeton, N.J.: Princeton University Press, 1972.

Riggs, A. R. "Penman of the Revolution: A Case for Arthur Lee." In *Essays in Early Virginia Literature Honoring Richard Beale Davis.* Ed. J. A. Leo Lemay. New York: Burt Franklin & Co., 1977. Pp. 203–19.

Robertson, John. *Opuscula, seria ac jocosa.* 3 numbers. N.p.: n.p., 1870–73. Copy at Huntington Library.

Robertson, Wyndham. *Pocahontas alias Matoaka, and Her Descendants.* Ed. R[obert] A. Brock. 1887; rpt. Baltimore: Genealogical Publishing Co., 1968.

Rouse, Alice Riddle Read. *The Reads and Their Relations.* Cincinnati: Johnson & Hardin Press, 1930.

Rouse, Parke, Jr. *James Blair of Virginia.* Chapel Hill: University of North Carolina Press, 1971.

Rowlandson, Mary. *The Soveraignty & Goodness of God . . . Being a Narrative of the Captivity and Restauration of Mrs. Mary Rowlandson* [1682]. In Robert K. Diebold. "A Critical Edition of Mrs. Mary Rowlandson's Captivity Narrative." Ph.D. diss., Yale University, 1972.

Rutman, Darrett B., and Anita H. Rutman. "Of Agues and Fevers: Malaria in the Early Chesapeake." *William and Mary Quarterly*, 3d ser., 33 (1976): 31–60.

Sabine, Lorenzo. *Biographical Sketches of Loyalists of the American Revolution.* 2 vols. Boston: Little, Brown, 1864.

Sanchez-Saavedra, E. M. *A Guide to Virginia Military Organizations in the American Revolution, 1774–1787.* Richmond: Virginia State Library, 1978.

Schutz, John A., ed. "A Private Report of General Braddock's Defeat." *Pennsylvania Magazine of History and Biography* 79 (1955): 374–77.

Seelye, John. *Prophetic Waters: The River in Early American Life and Literature.* New York: Oxford University Press, 1977.

Sewall, Samuel. *The Diary of Samuel Sewall.* Ed. M. Halsey Thomas. 2 vols. New York: Farrar, Straus and Giroux, 1973.

Shorter, Edward. *The Making of the Modern Family.* New York: Basic Books, 1975.

Shumsky, Neil Larry. "Parents, Children, and the Selection of Mates in Colonial Virginia." *Eighteenth-Century Life* 2 (1975): 83–88.

Slaughter, Philip. *A History of Bristol Parish, Va.* 2d ed. Richmond, Randolph & English, 1879.

Smith, Daniel Blake. *Inside the Great House: Planter Family Life in Eighteenth-*

Century Chesapeake Society. Ithaca, N.Y.: Cornell University Press, 1980.

————. "The Study of the Family in Early America: Trends, Problems, and Prospects." *William and Mary Quarterly,* 3d ser., 39 (1982): 1–28.

————, and Michael S. Hindus. "Premarital Pregnancy in America, 1640–1971: An Overview and Interpretation." *Journal of Interdisciplinary History* 5 (1975): 537–70.

Stanard, William G. "The Ancestors and Descendants of John Rolfe with Notices of Some Connected Families." *Virginia Magazine of History and Biography* 21 (1913): 105–6, 208–11, 222, 310–14, 422–27; 22 (1914): 103–7, 215–17, 331–33, 441–46; 23 (1915): 94–96, 214, 325–26, 441–43; 24 (1916): 94–97, 206–10, 327–33, 440–43.

————. "The Beverley Family." *Virginia Magazine of History and Biography* 20 (1912): 213–14, 332–33, 437–38; 21 (1913): 212–14, 305–6; 22 (1914): 102–3, 297–301.

————. "Harrison of James River." *Virginia Magazine of History and Biography* 34 (1926): 183–87.

————. "Major Robert Beverley and His Descendants." *Virginia Magazine of History and Biography* 2 (1894–95): 405–13; 3 (1895–96): 47–52, 169–76, 261–71, 383–92.

Stith, William. *The History of the First Discovery and Settlement of Virginia.* Williamsburg, Va.: W. Parks, 1747.

Stone, Lawrence. *Family, Sex, and Marriage in England, 1500–1700.* New York: Harper & Row, 1977.

Sweeny, William Montgomery, ed. *Marriage Bonds and Other Marriage Records of Amherst County, Va., 1763–1800.* Lynchburg, Va.: J. P. Bell Co., 1937.

Swem, Earl G. *Virginia Historical Index.* 2 vols. Roanoke, Va.: Stone Printing Co., 1934–36.

Tasso, Torquato. *Aminta.* Ed. Sarah D'Alberti. New York: S. T. Vanni, 1967.

————. *Aminta Englisht: The Henry Reynolds Translation.* Ed. Clifford Davidson. Fennimore, Wis.: John Weslburg, 1972.

————. *Il re Torrismondo.* Milano: Casa Editrice Sonzogno, [1921].

Terence. *Andria [The Lady of Andros; The Self-Tormenter; The Eunuch].* Tr. John Sargeaunt. Loeb Classical Library. Cambridge: Harvard University Press, 1912.

Thomas, Isaiah. *The History of Printing in America.* Ed. Marcus A. McCorison. New York: Weathervane Books, 1970.

Thompson, Roger. *Sex in Middlesex: Popular Mores in a Massachusetts County, 1649–1699.* Amherst: University of Massachusetts Press, 1986.

Thomson, Robert Polk. "The Tobacco Export of the Upper James River Naval District, 1773–75." *William and Mary Quarterly,* 3d ser., 18 (1961): 393–407.

Thwaites, Reuben Gold, and Louise Phelps Kellogg, eds. *Documentary History of Dunmore's War, 1774.* Madison: Wisconsin Historical Society, 1905.

Tinling, Marion, ed. *The Correspondence of the Three William Byrds of Westover, Virginia, 1684–1776.* 2 vols. Charlottesville: University Press of Virginia, 1977.

Torrence, Clayton. "The Petersons, Claibornes, and Harrisons, and Some of Their Connections." *William and Mary Quarterly,* 2d ser., 2 (1922): 1–19.

Truckell, A. E. "Early Shipping References in the Dumfries Burgh Records." *Dumfriesshire and Galloway Natural History & Antiquarian Society, Transactions* 33 (1954–55): 132–75; 34 (1955–56): 28–58.

Tucker, St. George. *The Poems of St. George Tucker of Williamsburg, Virginia, 1752–1827.* Ed. William S. Prince. New York: Vantage Press, 1977.

Turner, Susan McNeil. "The Skipwiths of Prestwould Plantation." *Virginia Calvacade* 10 (Summer 1960): 42–45.

Tyler, Lyon Gardiner. *Encyclopedia of Virginia Biography.* 5 vols. New York: Lewis Historical Publishing Co., 1915.

Valentine, Edward Pleasants. *Papers.* Ed. Clayton Torrence. 4 vols. Richmond: Valentine Museum, 1927.

Virgil. *Eclogues, Georgics, Aeneid I–IV.* Tr. H. Rushton Fairclough. 1916; rev. ed., Loeb Classical Library, Cambridge: Harvard University Press, 1978.

Von Closen, Ludwig. *The Revolutionary Journal of Baron Ludwig von Closen, 1780–1783.* Tr. and ed. Evelyn M. Acomb. Chapel Hill: University of North Carolina Press, 1958.

Voorhis, Manning C. "Bollingbrook." *William and Mary Quarterly,* 2d ser., 16 (1936): 545–53.

Warfield, J. Ogle. "Bolling Family Bible: Prince George County, Virginia." *Virginia Genealogist* 12 (1968): 33–34.

Warner, Charles Willard Hoskins. *Hoskins of Virginia and Related Families . . . Roy*. Tappahannock, Va.: n.p., 1971.

Warren, Mrs. J. E. "Notes on Roy, Beverly, Smith, and Allied Families." *Tyler's Quarterly Magazine* 18 (1936–37): 97–105, 175–89, 247–52.

Washington, Booker T. *Papers*. Vol. 1. *The Autobiographical Writings*. Ed. Louis R. Harlan and John W. Blassingame. Urbana: University of Illinois Press, 1972.

Washington, George. *Diaries*. Ed. Donald Jackson and Dorothy Twohig. 6 vols. Charlottesville: University Press of Virginia, 1976–79.

———. *Papers: Colonial Series*. Ed. W. W. Abbot. Charlottesville: University Press of Virginia, 1983–.

———. *Writings*. Ed. John C. Fitzpatrick. 39 vols. Washington, D.C.: U.S. Government Printing Office, 1931–44.

Watterson, John. "Poetic Justice; or, An Ill-fated Epic by Thomas Burke." *North Carolina Historical Review* 55 (1978): 339–44.

Weisiger, Benjamin B., III. "Prince George County, Virginia: Records, 1733–1792." N.p., 1975. Mimeographed. Copy at University of Virginia Library.

Wheeler, Robert. "The County Court in Colonial Virginia." In *Town and Country: Essays on the Structure of Local Government in the American Colonies*. Ed. Bruce C. Daniels. Middletown, Conn.: Wesleyan University Press, 1978. Pp. 111–33.

Whitelaw, Ralph T. *Virginia's Eastern Shore*. 2 vols. Richmond: Virginia Historical Society, 1951.

Whitley, Edythe Rucker. *Genealogical Records of Buckingham County, Virginia*. Baltimore: Genealogical Publishing Co., 1984.

Wulfeck, Dorothy Ford. "Marriages of Some Virginia Residents, 1607–1800." 7 vols. Naugatuck, Conn., 1961–67. Mimeographed. Copy at Local History and Genealogical Room, Library of Congress.

Wyatt, Edward Avery, IV. *Plantation Houses around Petersburg*. Petersburg, Va.: n.p., 1955.

Zuckerman, Michael. "William Byrd's Family." *Perspectives in American History* 12 (1979): 253–311.

Index

Index

First-Line Index to Bolling's Poems